# Literacy in Action

## Authors

Dr. Sharon Jeroski

Andrea Bishop
Jean Bowman
Lynn Bryan
Linda Charko
Maureen Dockendorf
Christine Finochio
Jo Ann Grime
Joanne Leblanc-Haley
Deirdre McConnell
Carol Munro
Cathie Peters
Lorraine Prokopchuk
Arnold Toutant

**PEARSON**

Education
Canada

**Grade 4 Project Team**

Team Leader: Anita Borovilos
National Literacy Consultant: Norma MacFarlane
Publisher: Susan Green
Product Manager: Donna Neumann
Managing Editor: Gaynor Fitzpatrick
Sr. Developmental Editor: Anne MacInnes
Editor: Kathleen ffolliott
Production/Copy Editor: Jessica Westhead
Production Coordinator: Zane Kaneps
Art Director: Zena Denchik
Designers: Zena Denchik and Carolyn Sebestyen
Permissions Research: Cindy Howard
Photo Research: Christina Beamish and Cindy Howard
Vice-President Publishing and Marketing: Mark Cobham

ISBN 0-13-201734-2 (softcover)
ISBN 0-13-204663-6 (hardcover)

Printed and bound in Canada.
1 2 3 4 5   TC   10 09 08 07 06

The publisher has taken every care to meet or exceed industry
specifications for the manufacturing of textbooks. The cover of this sewn
book is a premium, polymer-reinforced material designed to provide long life
and withstand rugged use. Mylar gloss lamination has been applied for
further durability.

PEARSON

Education
Canada

# Acknowledgements

## Series Consultants

Andrea Bishop
Anne Boyd
Christine Finochio
Joanne Leblanc-Haley

Don Jones
Jill Maar
Joanne Rowlandson
Carole Stickley

## Specialist Reviewers

Science: Doug Herridge
  Toronto, ON
Social Studies: Marg Lysecki
  Toronto, ON
Aboriginal: Ken Ealey
  Edmonton, AB

Equity: Dianna Mezzarobba
  Vancouver, BC
Levelling: Iris Zammit
  Toronto, ON

## Grades 3–6 Advisors and Reviewers

Dr. Frank Serafini
  Assistant Professor,
  University of Las Vegas,
  Las Vegas, Nevada

Patricia Adamson
  Winnipeg, MB
Marion Ahrens
  Richmond Hill, ON
Sandra Ball
  Surrey, BC
Gwen Bartnik
  Vancouver, BC
Jennifer Batycky
  Calgary, AB
Michelle Bellavia
  Hamilton, ON
Mary-Jane Black
  Hamilton, ON
Jackie Bradley
  Saskatoon, SK
Diane Campbell
  Durham, ON
Nancy Carl
  Coquitlam, BC
Janet Chow
  Burnaby, BC
Marla Ciccotelli
  London, ON
Susan Clarke
  Burlington, ON
Norma Collinson
  Truro, NS
Lynn Crews
  Lower Sackville, NS

Kathryn D'Angelo
  Richmond, BC
Susan Elliott
  Toronto, ON
Diane Gagley
  Calgary, AB
Michael Gallant
  Calgary, AB
Jennifer Gardner
  Vernon, BC
Adrienne Gear
  Vancouver, BC
Faye Gertz
  Niska, AB
Cindy Gordon
  Victoria, BC
Kathleen Gregory
  Victoria, BC
James Gray
  Winnipeg, MB
Myrtis Guy
  Torbay, Newfoundland
Kim Guyette-Carter
  Dartmouth, NS
Jackie Hall
  Vancouver, BC
Natalie Harnum
  Berwick, NS
Deborah Holley
  Duncan, BC
Joanne Holme
  Surrey, BC
Patricia Horstead
  Maple Ridge, BC
Carol Hryniuk-Adamov
  Winnipeg, MB

Pamela Jacob
  Limestone, ON
Joanne Keller
  Delta, BC
Dawn Kesslering
  Regina, SK
Karen Quan King
  Toronto, ON
Linda Kirby
  Sault Ste. Marie, ON
Sheryl Koers
  Duncan, BC
Roger Lacey
  Calgary, AB
Caroline Lutyk
  Burlington, ON
Heather MacKay
  Richmond, BC
Margaret Marion
  Niagara Falls, ON
Sangeeta McAuley
  Toronto, ON
Paula McIntee
  Allanburg, ON
Caroline Mitchell
  Guelph, ON
Laura Mossey
  Durham, ON
Rhonda Nixon
  Edmonton, AB
Gillian Parsons
  Brantford, ON
Linda Perrin
  Saint John, NB
Charolette Player
  Edmonton, AB

Rhonda Rakimov
  Duncan, BC
Tammy Reynard
  Duncan, BC
Kathryn Richmond
  St. Catharines, ON
Kristine Richards
  Windsor, ON
Barbara Rushton
  New Minas, NS
Jaye Sawatsky
  Delta, BC
Michelle Sharratt
  Woodbridge, ON
Cathy Sheridan
  Ottawa, ON
Nanci-Jane Simpson
  Hamilton, ON
Kim Smith
  Newmarket, ON
Candace Spilsbury
  Duncan, BC
Patricia Tapp
  Hamilton, ON
Vera Teschow
  Mississauga, ON
Joanne Traczuk
  Sutton West, ON
Susan Wilson
  St. Catharines, ON
Sonja Willier
  Edmonton, AB
Kelly Winney
  London, ON
Beth Zimmerman
  London, ON

# CONTENTS

# What Is Courage? • 2

## Read Together

## Shared

Learn Together Poster

## Guided Practice

## Literacy in Action

## Independent Practice

## Read! Write! Say! Do!

### Your Literacy Portfolio

# Get the Message! • 56

## View Together

## Shared

Learn Together Poster

## Guided Practice

**Images with Impact**
  *by Cathie Peters*  (posters)

## Literacy in Action

## Independent Practice

## Read! Write! Say! Do!

hug

## Your Literacy Portfolio

# UNIT 3

# Survivors! • 116

## Read Together

## Shared

*Learn Together Poster*

## Guided Practice

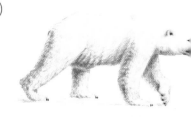

## Literacy in Action

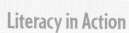

## Independent Practice

## Read! Write! Say! Do!

## Your Literacy Portfolio

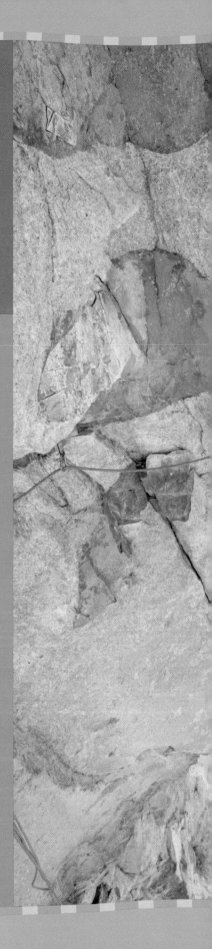

# What Is Courage?

## LEARNING GOALS

In this unit you will:

- Read, listen to, and talk about real-life stories about courage.

- Make connections to your own life and to other stories.

- Analyze who is included in media stories about courage.

- Write and tell recounts about real-life events.

speaking up
being yourself
trying again
facing your mistakes
being a hero

3

# Mia's Problem

by Sandra McLeod Humphrey

Illustrated by Diane Dawson Hearn

What kind of problem makes Mia look for courage?

My name's Mia and my problem began last Thursday. That's when Ms. Bradshaw, our language arts teacher, told our class that we had to finish up our book reports by Monday and be ready to give our oral book reports.

The good news is that we could choose any book. The bad news is that I don't read books.

Why should I read books when I can learn just as much from watching TV? And why should I worry about learning how to write when I can talk? If we're talking about real communication here, anyone knows that you can say a lot more and in much less time by talking than by writing.

There are a lot of things I *do* like about school— like recess and lunch and gym class and field trips and a whole bunch of other things. I just don't like to read books or write papers.

And I especially don't like to give speeches. It's not that I'm all that shy, I just don't like having to stand up there in front of the whole class and talk.

My heart starts pounding double-time, my hands get all sweaty, and my mouth is so dry that I can hardly talk.

Anyway, Ms. Bradshaw assigned us to teams, with three kids to a team. Both the kids on my team are really smart. They both read the book in one night. It took me three days to get through it.

Aaron can really draw, so he did all the pictures for the book report. And Katie is a computer whiz, so she offered to type our report for us.

That left me to do the oral report! All weekend I thought about nothing else. Videos kept running through my head: twenty million different ways how I could mess up!

I was hoping that by Monday I could come down with some kind of weird illness that would keep me home. But no such luck!

Monday came and I didn't even have the sniffles. So that's why I'm sitting here in my math class counting the dots on the boy's shirt in front of me.

While Mrs. Marcus is talking about fractions, I'm still trying to think of ways to get out of doing the oral book report.

It's bad enough looking like a fool on my own, but this time I'm part of a team and the grades for our report will depend on *all* of us. What a bummer!

As I head to my next class, I feel like I'm walking into the doctor's office to get a flu shot.

I'm taking a last drink at the water fountain before going into class when Russell calls out to me from down the hall.

"Hey, Mia, are you ready for Ms. Bradshaw's class? You don't look too good! Are you all right?"

I'm thinking that Russell is right. I probably look as lousy as I feel, so why not head upstairs to the nurse's office? It would be easy to fake a stomach ache. Or maybe I could actually throw up.

But if I chicken out today, that just means I'll have to give the report tomorrow, and that really doesn't solve my problem.

So what do I do? Fake a natural disaster or take a deep breath and get the report over with? There's something to be said for getting it over with, even if it means letting my team down.

Meanwhile, Russell's staring at me like he's waiting for me to make up my mind. Do I go into class with him or take the easy way out and head for the nurse's office?

## LET'S TALK ABOUT IT...

- What do you think Mia will do? Why? How does it take courage to deal with a problem like this?

- Role-play a time at school that made you or other students worry like Mia did. Show what courage looks and sounds like.

# Read About Real-Life Events

Real-life events are true stories that really happened. Think about a real-life event you enjoyed reading about or watching on TV.

- What was it about?
- Why did you like it?
- How was it different from a made-up story?

## TALK ABOUT IT!

- Share your real-life event with a partner or a group.
- Talk about where you can find true stories about real-life events.

Here are some clues.

Make a chart together.

True Stories About Real-Life Events

| Where you can find them | Examples |
|---|---|
| | |

# Think Like a Reader

- Why do you read about real-life events?

## Crack the code

Here are some words that can help you read and write about courage. What strategies can help you read them?

▲ determination
dangerous

risking
bravery

## Make meaning

Practise using these strategies when you read about real-life events:

**PREDICT**

Look at the headings and pictures for clues. What do you predict will happen?

**PAUSE AND CHECK**

As you read, think about your predictions. Were you right? Make new predictions about what will happen next.

**CONNECT**

Think about how the story relates to what has happened to you in your own life.

## Analyze what you read

- Why do you think people write about real-life events?
- Would two people writing about the same event tell the story in the same way? Why or why not?

# Trapped in Big Beaver

## PREDICT

Who do you think was trapped? Who showed courage?

## The Accident

James Amell and his family live in Big Beaver, Saskatchewan. One day, James and his sister Neely were sitting in their dad's truck. They were waiting for their dad to fix a tire on a combine in the field. Suddenly, James and his sister heard their dad scream. "Get this thing off of me!" he yelled.

James and Neely ran to see what was wrong. Their dad was pinned under the combine! It had fallen on one of his legs! James and his sister tried to lift it up and free him. But they weren't strong enough. That's when James's dad told James he would have to take the truck and go find help.

James sits in the truck that he drove when he went for help.

# James to the Rescue

James knew his dad was right, but he was scared. He had driven the truck in the field back home. But he had never driven the truck by himself—and never on the road.

James climbed up into the driver's seat. He couldn't even reach the pedals. He moved the driver's seat as far forward as he could. Then, he sat on the edge of the seat. Now his feet could reach the pedals.

He started the truck. His dad told him where he would find a neighbour's farmhouse. James drove eight kilometres before he found it. There was no one home! He went back to his father, who told him how to get to another farmhouse. When James found it, this time there were people there who could help him.

**PAUSE AND CHECK**

How will James rescue his dad?

A combine is a farm machine. It is used to harvest grain.

# A Hero Is Born

When James and the neighbours got back to the accident scene, they worked together to lift the combine. Then they moved his dad to safety. They also called an ambulance. His dad had a broken leg, but he would be okay.

The story of the eight-year-old who drove a truck to rescue his father was soon on the news. It was on TV, on the Internet, and in newspapers across Canada. James was a hero. His bravery saved the day.

James and his dad after the rescue.

11

**CONNECT**

How does James's story remind you of other stories you know?

# A New Beginning

**PREDICT**

How might a new student need courage?

## A New Country, A New School

Seema Mohammad-Essa was starting another school year. How different she felt from her first day at school three years ago!

Seema and her family had escaped from war-torn Afghanistan when she was two years old. Then they lived in Pakistan for five years. She moved to Canada with her mother and brothers in 2003. She was then able to go to school for the very first time.

Seema (left) plays with a friend in the yard at her school in Hamilton, Ontario.

12

Seema remembered how scared she was on that first day. At recess, she thought that the children playing in the yard were the teachers' children. Everything she saw, did, or heard was so different from what she had known.

## Ignoring Fear

The children in her class were all strangers to her. She couldn't talk to them because she didn't know how to speak English. But she decided that she would not let her fear stop her from speaking.

Slowly, Seema began to learn English. She learned the words *go* and *come* from a cartoon. She would put up her hand and say "go" and "come" to the teacher when he called her name. She was proud that she could say words in English. She felt bad, though, when some of the other students stared at her. Still, she kept practising and using new English words.

## Looking to the Future

Seema has never forgotten how it feels to be at school in a new country. She dreams that one day she will become a police officer. "I could help people when they don't know the language," she says. "I could help them to understand. Then they would feel less afraid as they start their new life in Canada."

Seema and her family immigrated to Canada from Pakistan on May 13, 2003.

**PAUSE AND CHECK**

How will Seema get over being scared?

Seema translates for a student who is learning English.

**CONNECT**

How does Seema's story remind you of other stories you know?

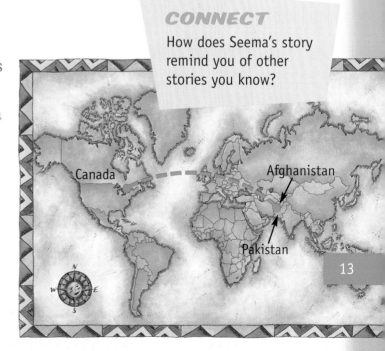

13

# As Good as Gold

## Going for Gold

Silken Laumann sat in her **scull** preparing to race. Just ten
weeks earlier, she had been rammed by another scull in a
training accident. Her leg below the knee was broken so badly
that doctors told her she would never row again. But here she
was, about to row the race of her life at the Barcelona
Summer Olympic Games. Would only four weeks of training
before the race be enough to help her win the gold medal?

Silken on race day at
the 1992 Summer
Olympics in
Barcelona, Spain.

# What Is a Single Scull?

A single scull is a rowing frame designed for one person. It is 8.2 m long, and very narrow.

The boat's seat is on wheels that run on tracks. The rower faces backwards, with the seat closest to the rear of the boat.

The rower pushes the seat forward with her legs as she pulls the oars through the water. Repeating this motion makes the boat go quickly.

## PAUSE AND CHECK

How do you think the race will end?

## The Race Begins!

She waited to hear the starting gun. Every muscle in her body was ready to power her scull from the start line to the finish line. The crowd hushed. The Canadian fans watched nervously. Then the shot! All the rowers exploded from the starting gates. The race was underway!

Silken rowed the first half of the race as though she had never been injured. Then, at the halfway mark, she began to feel her lack of fitness. For a moment, she was so tired she didn't even think she could make it to the end. She fell to fourth spot.

## An Amazing Comeback

What did she choose to do? Later she would describe it this way: "I went crazy. I just kind of put my oars in the water and gave it everything I could for the last 20, 30 strokes of the race." Her effort made the difference. Silken won a bronze medal.

Laumann may have finished third, but she instantly became a Canadian sporting legend. In Barcelona she showed the world what courage and determination can do.

Silken received the bronze medal for single sculls at the 1992 Summer Olympics in Barcelona, Spain.

15

## CONNECT

How does Silken's story remind you of other stories you know?

# Reflect on Your Reading

**You have . . .**

- talked about courage.
- read real-life stories about courage.
- explored words and phrases that tell about courage.

I think courage is when you are scared to do something, but you do it anyway. What do **you** think?

afraid    scared    heroism    determination    bravery    believe in yourself    risking

**You have also . . .**

- explored different reading strategies.

**PREDICT**
**PAUSE**
**AND CHECK**
**CONNECT**

## Write About Learning

Write about one of the strategies you used when you read the selection "Acts of Courage." How did the strategy help you read and understand the selection? Tell how the strategy might help you when you read other kinds of stories.

# Read Like a Writer

When you were reading "Acts of Courage," you were reading *recounts*. A recount tells a series of events. It is one of the most common forms of talking, writing, and representing.

## TALK ABOUT IT!

- What do you notice about the way recounts are written?

- Make a chart to show what you know about recounts. Add to the chart as you read and write more recounts of your own.

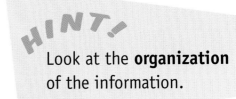

**HINT!**

Look at the **organization** of the information.

Recounts

- tell what happened in order
- usually use action words in the past tense
- use describing words to make events interesting
- tell who, where, when, what, how

# Catch the Dream

by CTV news staff

**READ LIKE A WRITER**

How does information in the first paragraph catch readers' interest?

How could someone catch a dream on a mountain in Africa?

18

## A Dream Is Born

It's the roof of Africa. As the highest point on the African continent, Mount Kilimanjaro is considered a sacred place. Half a world away, Wendy Bigcharles and Laurie Gaucher are making plans to climb the mountain. They are Cree from Sucker Creek in northern Alberta. They want to climb the mountain for every Aboriginal child in Canada.

"I think we have to get out there as Aboriginal people and start showing each other what we're capable of doing," says Wendy.

Wendy and Laurie plan to climb the highest mountains on each of the seven continents. Their idea is called "The Ascent of the Aboriginal Spirit." In between each expedition, they will travel around to share their stories with Aboriginal children.

"We want the children to know, 'You can do whatever you want to do. Don't let anybody tell you anything different. Just believe in yourself,'" says Laurie.

## Living the Dream

After raising money for the expedition, they head off on their adventure, even though Laurie is recovering from a broken ankle. It will be a gruelling 36-hour journey to the northeastern tip of Tanzania. Wendy and Laurie have two days to adjust to a new time zone, catch up on sleep, and get used to the heat.

They are excited, but still worried about Laurie's ankle. They are also worried about altitude sickness. The lack of oxygen and lower air pressure causes everything from mild headaches to death. Wendy fell ill in South America at 4900 m because of altitude sickness. If she gets sick again, will she be able to push through to the top of the mountain?

Mount Kilimanjaro's snow-capped peak is 5895 m above sea level.

Mount Kilimanjaro is in northeast Tanzania.

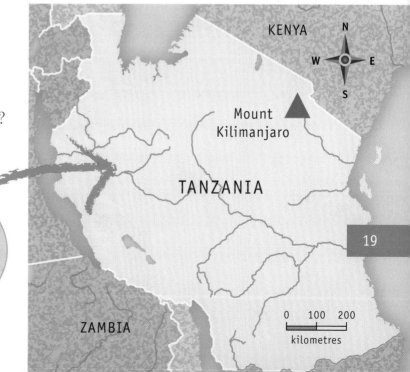

KENYA

Mount Kilimanjaro

TANZANIA

ZAMBIA

0   100   200
kilometres

| Facts About Mount Kilimanjaro | |
| --- | --- |
| Elevation | 5895 m |
| Location | Tanzania |
| Latitude | 3° 04' S |
| Longitude | 37° 21' E |
| Best months for climbing | December, January, February, March, June, July, August |

## DAY ONE

It's late in the day when Wendy and Laurie begin their trip. According to their guide Tom, they have to climb for at least four hours. The temperature is over 35°C.

"I feel it, but it's not hurting. I've got a headache. The heat doesn't agree with me," says Wendy.

It's the end of the first day, which is supposed to be the easiest.

## DAY TWO: 2400 m

The second day is like the first, five hours of uphill hiking. Tom decides the group is walking too fast. He will now walk in front and set a slow pace to train the group to walk at high altitude.

## DAY THREE: 3400 m

It's another four or five hours of climbing for the group.

## DAY FOUR: 4000 m

As the day goes on, both Wendy and Laurie begin to feel the altitude. Wendy can't keep any food or water down. Laurie is also feeling sick and his ankle is hurting. There are only 24 hours to get ready for the final climb.

Laurie takes a break on his way up Mount Kilimanjaro.

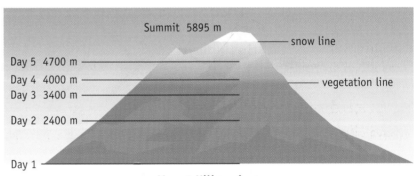

**Mount Kilimanjaro**

This diagram shows how high Wendy and Laurie were when they began their climb each day.

## DAY FIVE: 4700 m

It's summit day on Kilimanjaro. As the day passes, Wendy and Laurie start to get their strength back. By evening, they are both feeling well enough to try and reach the summit. The final ascent begins at midnight.

Just past 5500 m, their worst fear comes true. Laurie collapses and can go no further.

Now Wendy is faced with a hard decision. Does she take Laurie down the mountain? Does she pursue the dream? Wendy doesn't have much time to decide. She's losing body heat every minute. After much soul searching, Wendy decides to go on. As Laurie is helped down, she watches him disappear into the dark.

"By the time I got to the partial summit, at around 5800 m, my lungs were just so tight. There was pain ripping my whole chest. I didn't even have the energy to talk. The last two hours to the summit were excruciating pain," she says.

Despite everything, shortly after 8 a.m. Wendy makes the summit. She can only stay ten minutes because of the altitude. It is just enough time to perform a special task. She scatters some traditional herbs, and says a prayer. The dream is now complete.

**Wendy reaches the summit on Day 6 of the climb.**

## DIG DEEPER

1. Make a chart. List the challenges that the climbers faced and tell how they met each challenge.

| Challenges | How they met them |
|------------|-------------------|
|            |                   |

2. Imagine that you went with the climbers. With a partner, take turns interviewing each other about your experiences and accomplishments.

# Charlie's Story

## by Charles Ecclestone

How did Charlie's courage help him win a battle?

My name is Charles Ecclestone, but I like to be called Charlie. I am ten years old and I live with my Mom and Dad, my younger brother, Steven, and my younger sister, Jennifer. I have a cat, too, called Amber. I like karate, hanging out with friends, swimming, camping, basketball, and phys. ed. class.

When I was three, right after I started Junior Kindergarten, I began to get headaches. Some days I would come home from school and flop down on the couch and not eat any lunch. My parents took me to the doctor because they knew something was wrong. We went many times, and saw many doctors. Most doctors thought I had the flu. One doctor thought I was faking it because I didn't want to go to school! While all this was going on, my brother was born. Only five days after he was born, we found out what was making me sick. I had leukemia.

LEUKEMIA IS HORRIBLE. Leukemia is a cancer of your blood. My bone marrow was making more bad cells than good cells, and the bad cells were crowding out the good ones.

I had to go into the hospital right away to start my treatment, called chemotherapy, or "chemo" for short. I don't remember much about my time in the hospital, but I remember that some of the treatments really hurt!

Chemotherapy is good because it poisons and kills the bad cells. But chemo also makes you feel really sick and it changes the way you look. I became bald, just like my Grandpa John. Once when Grandpa John was staying with me in the hospital, we both looked in the mirror. Two bald heads stared out at us!

**READ LIKE A WRITER**
What words and phrases does Charlie use to tell readers when or how often things happened?

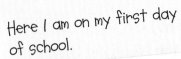
Here I am on my first day of school.

Sometimes I painted at home on the days I couldn't go to school.

23

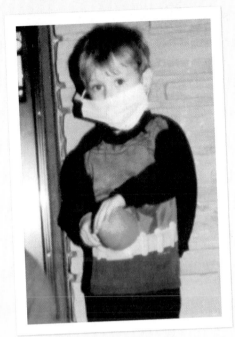

I'm wearing a mask to protect me from germs.

My sister often cheered me up by playing with me.

While I was having chemo, I had to be really careful that I didn't pick up germs from anyone. Sometimes I had to wear a mask if I was going to be around other people. Many days I couldn't go to school. I missed being able to see my friends. In Grade 2, I set a school record for the most days absent— 43 days! I still ended up near the top of my class, though.

For almost four years, I went in and out of the hospital, having chemo, blood tests, and needles. Sometimes I just didn't want to have even one more needle! I would scream, kick, and punch. But I would have my treatment anyway. My dad says I was amazingly strong. I always tried to be brave.

I eventually became a kind of celebrity. My picture was in the paper nine times. It was even on the front page! I was interviewed on television three times and on the radio once. There was also an article in a magazine about me. One day I was walking in a parking lot and a woman recognized me from the newspaper!

The Sunshine Foundation is a group that grants wishes to kids who are seriously ill. One day we found out that the Foundation was giving our whole family a holiday at Disney World. We had special passes that meant we didn't have to wait in any line-ups to go on the rides. I even had a private photo shoot with Mickey Mouse!

Every summer, my family and I go to Camp Trillium, a summer camp for kids who have been touched by cancer and their families. Last summer my sister and I went to the camp for eleven days by ourselves. I did a lot of fun stuff like fishing, archery, and swimming. At camp I got to meet other kids from all over Ontario. Some of the kids are fighting cancer. Some of them are the brothers and sisters of kids with cancer.

It's been three years since my last chemo treatment. After my last treatment, my class at school had a huge party to celebrate. We went swimming and watched a movie. The kids in my class gave me cards and gifts. There was pizza, garbage bags stuffed with popcorn, and an amazing cake that had "Nice Going" written on it.

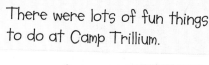

There were lots of fun things to do at Camp Trillium.

Here is the cake my friends at school gave me.

Every few months, I still need to go for blood tests to make sure that the bad cells haven't come back. When I have gone five years without needing any treatment, we are going back to Disney World. I know that in many ways I have been very lucky.

The scar on my chest from where the nurses gave me my medicine reminds me of what I had to go through when I had chemo. I think that going through chemo has made me more mature than most kids my age. I have learned that the little problems that upset some people are not really as important as they seem. I have learned what a bad day *really* is.

When I grow up, I'm going to be a lawyer. Lawyers have to fight hard to win their cases in court. With help from doctors, nurses, and my family, I fought cancer and I won. I think I will be a great lawyer!

## DIG DEEPER ·············································

1. Write a letter to Charlie telling him what you learned about courage from his story.

2. Why do you think people who choose stories for newspapers, radio, and TV selected Charlie's story to tell? Why is his story important? Share your ideas in a group.

# Pictures of
# Courage

by Anne Bannerjee

We all have moments in
our lives when we are called
upon to show courage.

How can a photograph tell about courage?

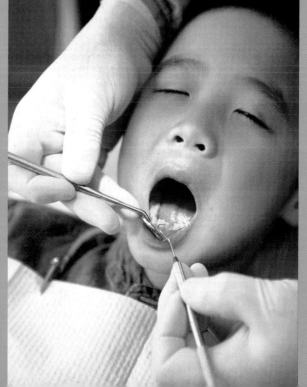

Find pictures of courage in newspapers and magazines. What kinds of courage do they show?

## DIG DEEPER

1. Choose the photograph that has the strongest message about courage for you. Write about how it connects to your life and your ideas.

2. Find a photo that shows courage. The photo can be from home or from a newspaper, magazine, book, or Web site. Write a caption for your photo. Share it with a group.

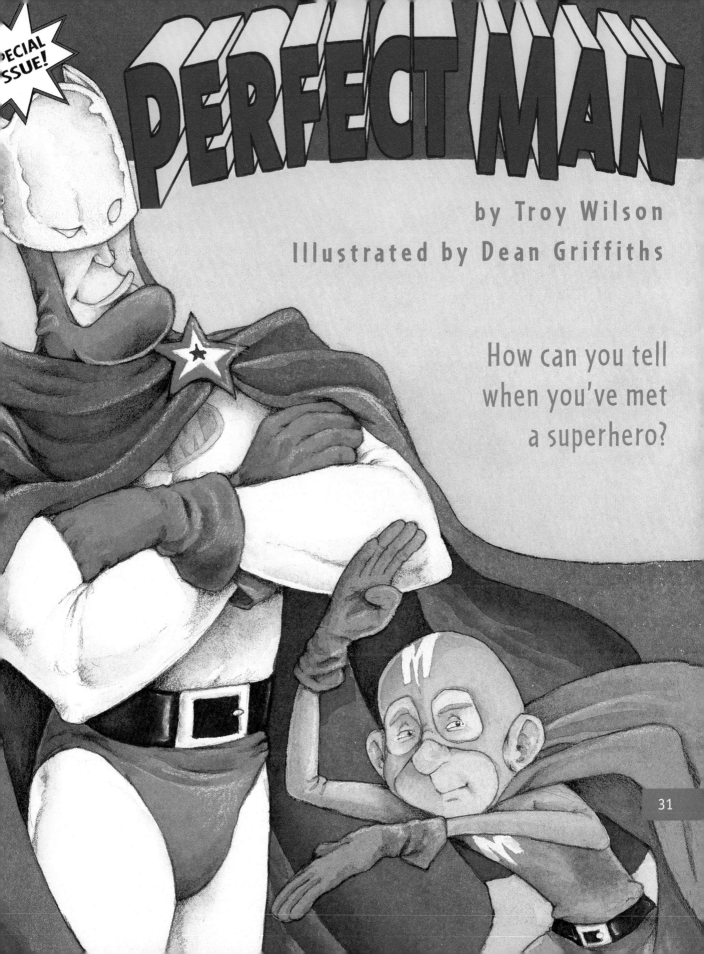

# PERFECT MAN

by Troy Wilson

Illustrated by Dean Griffiths

How can you tell
when you've met
a superhero?

**READ LIKE A WRITER**

How does Troy Wilson use details to show his readers how much Michael likes Perfect Man?

Michael Maxwell McAllum was the smallest boy in his class. He lived in a small house in a small town on a small street. Sometimes he went on trips with his family.

Perfect Man was the greatest superhero of them all. He lived…well…no one knows where he lived. Sometimes he went to other dimensions.

Michael Maxwell McAllum was Perfect Man's biggest fan.

He covered his walls with Perfect Man posters. He read Perfect Man comics and played Perfect Man video games. He ate Perfect Man cereal and wore Perfect Man T-shirts.

He watched Perfect Man on the six o'clock news. He cut Perfect Man out of the newspaper. He wrote Perfect Man stories. He made a Perfect Man Web site.

Before he went to sleep each night, he turned out his
Perfect Man lamp. He dreamed about Perfect Man.

Perfect Man,

    Perfect Man,

        Perfect Man.

And then Perfect Man quit.

Just like that. He said it was time for a change. He
said it was time to start a new chapter in his life.

"Who will save the world when you're gone?" the
reporters asked.

"I used to be the only superhero around," Perfect
Man said. "These days, it's hard to keep track of them all.
They'll do just fine without me."

"What's your secret identity?"

Perfect Man smiled. "If I told you, it wouldn't be
much of a secret, would it?"

"Where will you go?"

"Someplace quiet," Perfect Man said.

"What will you do?"

"Oh, I'll find something. After
all, there's more than one way
to save the world."

"You must be so sad," Michael's mother said. "You must feel like you've lost your best friend."

She didn't understand. She didn't know Perfect Man like he did. Perfect Man would come back. Just like the time he came back from deep space when he escaped the cosmic pirates. Just like the time he came back from Dimension Z when he beat Zrog the Unbeatable. Just like the time he came back from the dead when he...well...died. He *always* came back. Always.

That summer, Michael Maxwell McAllum watched on TV as aliens invaded New York.

They always invaded New York. They never invaded his small town. The Amazing Five teamed up with the Super Squadron to stop them.

Perfect Man will come back, he thought.

Summer ended.

Michael Maxwell McAllum went back to school.

And Perfect Man came back. Just like that. Perfect Man had changed. Michael didn't recognize him at first. He wasn't wearing his costume anymore. His hair was thinner. His stomach was rounder. He didn't even call himself Perfect Man anymore. He called himself Mr. Clark.

He was Michael Maxwell McAllum's new teacher.

Mr. Clark never broke the chalk. He never lost his temper. And he never got sick.

When Mr. Clark talked about the planets, it seemed as if he had visited them himself.

When there was trouble in the schoolyard, Mr. Clark was there. When Alexander dropped his art project, Mr. Clark was there. He was everywhere at once. At least it seemed that way.

Mr. Clark was the fastest marker in the world. And, best of all, Mr. Clark looked inside people. He saw all the good stuff and helped them bring it out. He helped them find their super powers.

Michael Maxwell McAllum knew Mr. Clark was Perfect Man. He was sure of it. But he didn't post it on his Web site. He didn't tell Mom or Dad. He didn't tell anybody. Instead, he wrote a story about Perfect Man. In the story, Perfect Man became a teacher in a small town. Only one boy suspected his secret. When Perfect Man decided to fight crime again, he made the boy his sidekick.

Michael Maxwell McAllum gave the story to Mr. Clark.

"Well, that's an original story," Mr. Clark said. "It's the best Perfect Man story you've written yet. I think the ending could use a little work, though."

"I know you're Perfect Man," Michael said.

Mr. Clark smiled. "Do I look like Perfect Man?"

"You're disguised," Michael answered. "I remember how you kept Dr. Plasma's shape-changing machine when he went to jail. Or maybe your friend the Dark Avenger helped you out. He's a master of disguises."

"Those are good theories," said Mr. Clark.

"Am I right?" asked Michael.

Mr. Clark didn't say "yes" and he didn't say "no." He said, "If Perfect Man were here today, he'd tell you exactly what I'm telling you now. You don't need to be the sidekick, Michael. You can be the superhero."

"What do you mean?" asked Michael.

"You already have a super power," said Mr. Clark. "You have the power to write. You write very well."

"I guess I write okay…"

"No," Mr. Clark insisted. "You write very well. Do you like to write?"

Michael nodded.

"Then I hope you keep writing," said Mr. Clark. "I really do."

He paused. "Do you want to know a secret, Michael?"

Michael Maxwell McAllum leaned forward. "Yes. Yes, I do."

Only **one** boy suspected his secret.

He tried
new
things
and met
new
friends.

"To be a good writer, you have to read and you have to write," said Mr. Clark. "But there's another step. A secret step."

"What?" asked Michael. "What is it?"

"You have to live," said Mr. Clark. "You have to try new things. You have to meet new people. That's what good writers do. They live. And it's all research. Every second of it."

Michael leaned back. He thought for a second. Then he said, "I have one question."

"Yes?"

"What does flying feel like?"

Mr. Clark laughed. "Don't you have another story to write?" he said.

Michael Maxwell McAllum did have another story to write. He had a lot of other stories to write. Some of them were wonderful. Some of them were awful. And most were somewhere in between.

He tried new things and met new friends. He made new mistakes.

"It's research," he told himself over and over again. "It's all research."

He grew and he wrote and he lived.

Today Mr. Clark is still a teacher. He loves what he does. Sometimes he thinks about Perfect Man and smiles.

Michael Maxwell McAllum is a best-selling author. He loves what he does.

Mr. Clark is Michael Maxwell McAllum's biggest fan.

## MEDIA WATCH

Make a list of superheroes in TV and movies. What do you notice about the people on your list?

38

## DIG DEEPER

1. Create a new secret identity for Perfect Man. Include a sketch. Share your ideas with a group.

2. How would the story be different if Perfect Man were Perfect Woman?

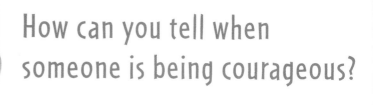

How can you tell when
someone is being courageous?

# 74th Street

by Myra Cohn Livingston

Hey, this little kid gets roller skates.
She puts them on.
She stands up and almost
flops over backwards.
She sticks out a foot like
she's going somewhere and
falls down and
smacks her hand. She
grabs hold of a step to get up and
sticks out the other foot and
slides about six inches and
falls and
skins her knee.

And then, you know what?

She brushes off the dirt and the
blood and puts some
spit on it and then
sticks out the other foot

*again.*

40

# Courage

**by Emily Hearn**

Courage is when you're
allergic to cats and
your new friend says can
you come to her house to
play after school and
stay to dinner then
maybe go skating and
sleep overnight. And,
she adds, you can pet
her small kittens. Oh,
how you ache to. It
takes courage to
say 'no' to all that.

**READ LIKE A WRITER**
How do the poets use details to
give their readers a strong
picture of what's happening?

## DIG DEEPER

1. With a group, practise reading and
   presenting one of the poems. Decide
   who will take each part. You can act it
   out, or just read the words.

2. Create a cartoon strip with four boxes
   that shows the story of **one** of the
   poems. Use speech balloons and
   thought bubbles.

41

# Writers at Work!

People often get special awards for showing courage.

Think of someone you know who deserves a courage award.

*Jaleen stood up for her brother when everyone was mad at him.*

## Choose Someone for the Award

- Think about a time when you saw someone show courage. It might be someone in your class, a family member, or even a pet.

- Remember, courage is not always about facing danger. Often, courage is about doing what's right, even when it is hard.

## Write About His or Her Courage

- Write the real-life story of his or her act of courage.

- Make a plan to organize your ideas.

- Recount what he or she did.

**VOICE**

- Show that you care about your topic.

- Include words or ideas that will stick in your readers' minds.

- End your recount by explaining why the person deserves an award for courage.
- Then work with a partner to improve your first draft.
- Remember to put "voice" in your writing.

## Design the Award

- What kind of award will you design?
- What pictures or symbols will you use to represent courage? Your award should give people a strong message about courage.

## Present the Award

- Think about how you will present your award.
- You could read your writing aloud to him or her, and then present the award.
- Whatever you do, don't forget to congratulate him or her!

43

# AKIAK

## by Robert J. Blake

How can an animal show courage?

# Day One

Akiak knew it. The other dogs knew it, too.

Some had run it many times and others had never run it at all. But not a dog wanted to be left behind.

It was Iditarod Race Day. Eighteen hundred kilometres of wind, snow, and rugged trail lay ahead, from Anchorage to Nome. Akiak had led the team through seven races and knew the trail better than any dog. She had brought them in fifth, third, and second, but had never won. She was ten years old now. This was her last chance. Now, they must win now.

Crack! The race was under way. One by one, fifty-eight teams took off for Nome.

## READ LIKE A WRITER

Find a part of the story where Robert J. Blake creates strong word pictures. How does he make you see and feel what is happening?

# Day Two

"Come on, old girl, show 'em how," Mick called. "Haw!"

Mick worked the sixteen-dog team through Akiak, calling "Haw!" when she needed the dogs to turn left, and "Gee!" to go right. Mick was the musher, but the team followed the lead dog. The team followed Akiak.

Through steep climbs and dangerous descents, icy waters and confusing trails, Akiak always found the safest and fastest way. She never got lost.

# Day Three

Akiak and Squinty, Big Boy and Flinty, Roscoe and the rest of the team pounded across the snow for three days. The dogs were ready to break out, but Mick held them back. There was a right time—but not yet.

High in the Alaskan range they caught up to Willy Ketcham in third place. It was his team that had beaten them by just one minute last year. Following the rules, Willy pulled over and allowed Mick's team to pass.

"That old dog will never make it!" he laughed at Akiak across the biting wind.

"She'll be waiting for you at Nome!" Mick vowed.

# Day Four

High in the Kuskokwim Mountains they passed Tall Tim Broonzy's team and moved into second place. Just after Takotna, Mick's team made its move. They raced by Whistlin' Perry's team to take over first place.

Ketcham made his move, too. His team clung to Mick's like a shadow.

Akiak and her team now had to break trail through deep snow. It was tough going. By the Ophir checkpoint, Akiak was limping. The deep snow had jammed up one of her pawpads and made it sore. Mick tended to her as Ketcham raced by and took first place from them.

"You can't run on that paw, old girl," Mick said to her. "With a day's rest it will heal, but the team can't wait here a day. We've got to go on without you. You'll be flown home."

Roscoe took Akiak's place at lead.

# Day Five

By morning most of the other dog teams had passed through the Ophir checkpoint. The wind was building and the pilot was in a hurry to leave. Akiak tore at the leash as the volunteer brought her to the airplane.

"Get that dog in," the pilot hollered. "I want to get out of here before the storm hits!"

Akiak jumped and pulled and snapped. All she wanted was to get back on the trail. To run. To win. Then all at once, the wind gusted, the plane shifted, and Akiak twisted out of the handler's grip. By the time they turned around she was gone.

# Day Six

Akiak ran while the storm became a blizzard. She knew that Mick and the team were somewhere ahead of her. The wind took away the scent and the snow took away the trail, but still she knew the way. She ran and she ran, until the blizzard became a whiteout. Then she could run no more. While Mick and the team took refuge in Galena, seven hours ahead, Akiak burrowed into a snowdrift to wait out the storm.

In the morning the mound of snow came alive, and out pushed Akiak.

# Day Seven

Word had gone out that Akiak was loose. Trail volunteers knew that an experienced lead dog would stick to the trail. They knew she'd have to come through Unalakleet.

She did. Six hours after Mick and the team had left, Akiak padded softly, cautiously, into the checkpoint. Her ears alert, her wet nose sniffed the air. The team had been there, she could tell.

Suddenly, cabin doors flew open. Five volunteers fanned out and tried to grab her. Akiak zigged around their every zag and took off down the trail.

"Call ahead to Shaktoolik!" a man shouted.

# Day Eight

At Shaktoolik, Mick dropped two more dogs and raced out, still six hours ahead of Akiak.

Hungry now—it had been two days since she had eaten—Akiak pounded over the packed trail. For thirst, she drank out of the streams, the ice broken through by the sled teams.

She struggled into Shaktoolik in the late afternoon. Three men spotted her and chased her right into the community hall, where some mushers were sleeping. Tables overturned and coffee went flying. Then one musher opened the back door and she escaped.

"Go find them, girl," he whispered.

At Koyuk, Akiak raided the mushers' discard pile for food. No one came after her. At Elim, people put food out for her. Almost everybody was rooting for Akiak to catch her team.

# Day Nine

Mick rushed into White Mountain twenty-two minutes behind Ketcham. Here the teams had to take an eight-hour layover to rest before the final dash for Nome. Mick dropped Big Boy and put young Comet in his place. The team was down to eight dogs with 124 kilometres to go.

Akiak pushed on. When her team left White Mountain at 6 P.M., Akiak was running through Golovin, just two hours behind. A crowd lined the trail to watch her run through the town.

# Day Ten

Screaming winds threw bitter cold at the team as they fought their way along the coast. Then, halfway to the checkpoint called Safety, they came upon a maze of snowmobile tracks. The lead dogs lost the trail.

Mick squinted through the snow, looking for a sign.

There. Going right. She recognized Ketcham's trail.

"Gee!" she called. Gee—go right.

But the dogs wouldn't go. They wandered about, tangling up the lines. Mick straightened them out and worked the team up the hill. At the top they stopped short. Something was blocking the trail.

"Akiak!" Mick called.

She ran to her usual spot at the harness, waiting to be hooked in.

"Sorry, old girl," Mick hugged her. "Rules say I can't put you back in harness. Get in the sled."

But instead, Akiak circled the lead dogs, pushing them and barking.

"What is it, girl?" Mick asked.

Akiak ran back down the hill.

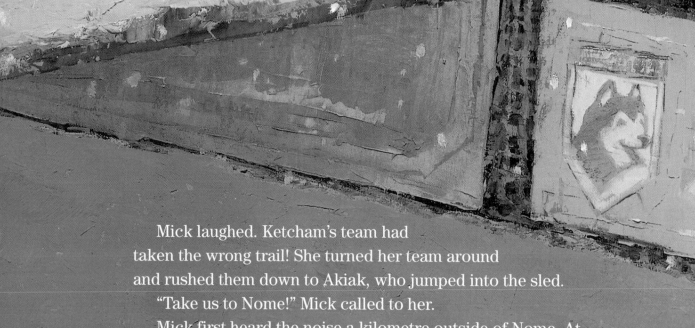

Mick laughed. Ketcham's team had taken the wrong trail! She turned her team around and rushed them down to Akiak, who jumped into the sled.

"Take us to Nome!" Mick called to her.

Mick first heard the noise a kilometre outside of Nome. At first she wasn't sure what it was. It grew so loud that she couldn't hear the dogs. It was a roar, or a rumble—she was so tired after ten days of mushing she couldn't tell which. Then she saw the crowd and she heard their cheers. People had come from everywhere to see the courageous dog that had run the Iditarod trail alone.

As sure as if she had been in the lead position, Akiak won the Iditarod Race.

"Nothing was going to stop this dog from winning," Mick told the crowd. Akiak knew it.

The other dogs knew it, too.

## DIG DEEPER

1. Write "Akiak" in the centre of a page. Make a web of words and phrases describing her. Use words in the story and others of your own.

2. With a group, make a list of stories you have read, heard, or seen where an animal showed courage. Talk about which stories "Akiak" is most like.

# Connect and Share

Most people like to tell stories about courage. They share stories at home and at school.

Now it's your turn to share.

## Take a story home!

- Choose a story from this unit.
- Practise telling it out loud.
- Tell it to someone you know.

## Bring a story back!

- Ask family members to tell you real-life stories of courage.
- The stories can be about people they know or events that happened in the news.
- Choose one story to share with a small group at school.

**PLANNING TIPS**

- Get the facts right.
- Tell things in order.
- Tell the most important parts.
- Have a beginning, middle, and end.

**PRESENTING TIPS**

- Practise so you don't forget what to say.
- Talk so everyone can hear.
- Use expression.

# Spotlight on **Learning**

## Collect

- Gather your notebooks, charts, cartoon strip, and other work you did in this unit.

## Talk and reflect

Work with a partner.

- Together, read the Learning Goals on page 2.
- Talk about how well you met these goals.
- Look through your work for evidence.

| My choices | I want this in my portfolio because... |
|---|---|
| | |

## Select

- Choose two pieces of work that show how you achieved the Learning Goals. (The same piece of work can show more than one goal.)

## Tell about your choices

- Tell what each piece shows about your learning.

## Reflect

- What have you learned about sharing real-life information?
- What have you discovered about courage?

55

# Get the
# Message!

## LEARNING GOALS

In this unit you will:

- View photographs and illustrations.
- Analyze how messages can be expressed through images.
- Think critically about visual messages.
- Use text and graphics to create strong messages.

communicate
images
body language
layout
message
symbols

57

# WHERE'S THE MESSAGE?

To: Squirt

From: Sis

Hey Squirt,

You've been getting messages all day. Look back and I'm sure you'll find them.

Sis

## LET'S TALK ABOUT IT...

- Identify all the messages you see in the cartoon strip.

- Which of the messages you see every day are most important to you?

# Viewing Messages

Many of the messages we send and receive include both words and images.

Sometimes it is mainly the image that catches our attention. Think about an ad, poster, or video game you have seen.

- What was the message?
- What were the images like?
- How did the images appeal to you?

## TALK ABOUT IT!

Work with a partner.

- What kinds of messages do you see around you every day?
- Talk about all the places you find them.

  Make a chart together.

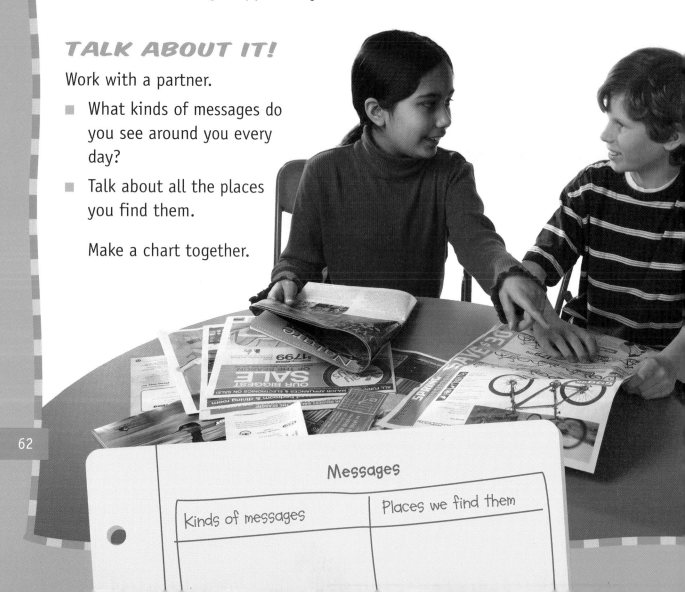

Messages

| Kinds of messages | Places we find them |
| --- | --- |
|  |  |

# Think Like a Viewer

**View with a purpose**

- Why do you look at images such as photographs?

**Crack the code**

Here are some questions that will help you when you look at images.

- What is the first thing you notice? What does it tell you about the message?
- How did the photographers make their work interesting?

**Make meaning**

Practise using these strategies when you view images:

| | |
|---|---|
| *USE WHAT YOU KNOW* | Ask yourself if the image reminds you of anything you have seen before. |
| *DECIDE WHAT'S IMPORTANT* | Ask yourself which parts are most important. What does the photographer want you to notice? |
| *EVALUATE* | Think about the message you see and how the photographer or artist helped you to find it. |

**Analyze what you see**

- How do people use images to change their audience's point of view or feelings?

KID

Power

65

COME ON! IT'S YOUR TURN!

Canada's **SCREAM**

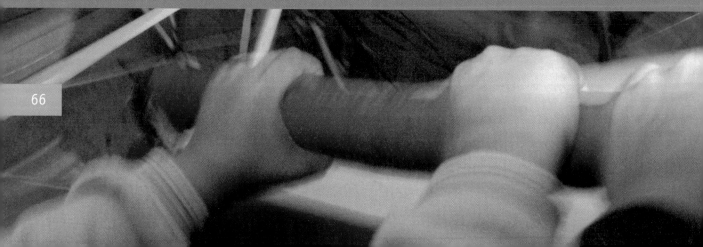

# MACHINES

TOTAL

PLEASE HELP US!
1 - PEOPLE
1 - DOG
1 - CAT

# DISASTER!

## HURRICANE KATRINA HITS HARD

# Reflect on Your Reading

**You have . . .**

- talked about messages.
- noticed how photographers use different kinds of camera shots.
- learned new vocabulary about viewing photographs.

I liked the close-up of the kids in the roller coaster car. You could tell how they were feeling from the expressions on their faces.

I liked the photos that showed kids helping in their communities. Even little kids can do their part.

layout

images

message

communicate

body language

symbols

**You have also . . .**

- explored different viewing strategies.

USE WHAT YOU KNOW

DECIDE WHAT'S IMPORTANT

EVALUATE

## Write About Learning

Write about one of the strategies you used to view and understand the poster. How did the strategy help you figure out the message? How could you use that strategy when you view other images?

# View Like a Photographer

When you were looking at "Images with Impact," you were viewing posters. Posters combine pictures, shapes, and words in different ways.

## TALK ABOUT IT!

- What do you notice about the way the posters are set up?
- Make a chart to show what you know about poster design.

HINT!

Look at the **presentation** of the information.

Posters

- have a large title
- have one or more photographs
- try to make you look at the most important thing first
- have some close-ups
- show parts of the message in every photograph

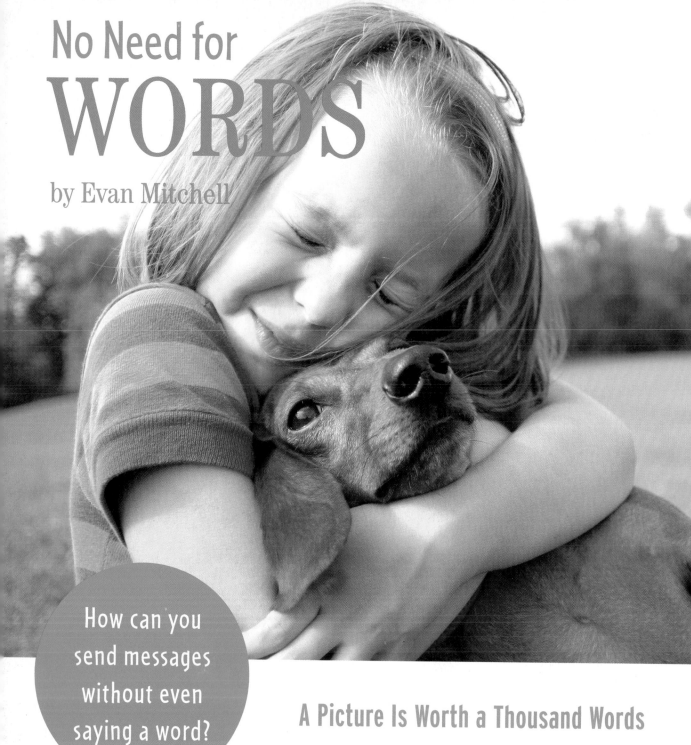

# No Need for
# WORDS

by Evan Mitchell

How can you send messages without even saying a word?

## A Picture Is Worth a Thousand Words

Every day, we make our feelings known without saying a word. Photographers try to capture emotions in a photo. You can read the photo by making a connection to your own life.

73

MEDIA WATCH

Find some photos of people in magazines or newspapers. What emotions do they show?

## DIG DEEPER

1. Suggest captions for these pictures. Explain why they are good captions.

2. With a partner, take turns silently acting out (miming) one of the expressions shown in the photos. Try to guess which photo your partner is acting out.

# TRICKY PICS

## How can you tell if a photo has been changed?

by Jamie Kiffel

When would a cat stick out its tongue at you? When it's an April Fool joke! The secret to that funny face on the right is called *photo manipulation*.

First the artist photographed Roswell the cat many times. Then he used computer tools to place images of the cat's paws onto its body—and its mouth. (It's like how you would make a photo collage.) But the tricky part was just getting the cat to open his mouth. "We needed a cat that meowed a lot," photographer John Lund says. "Luckily Roswell is a talker!" A computer tool stretched the image of the cat's mouth even more. The result? One funny photo!

### Bad to the Bone

The goggles never actually touched the real dogs' faces in this image. Photographer John Lund first took pictures of a human wearing them. Then he erased the human face using a computer and placed the goggles on the dogs.

# Eye DON'T Believe It

With computer programs such as Photoshop, just about anyone can change photographs. Digital artists use all sorts of tools and techniques. "Liquefying" tools help stretch smiles and bodies. A "radial zoom" effect blurs images so they look as if they are moving.

One of the most common techniques involves "cutting and pasting." Artists cut out part of one photo and paste it onto another. (That's how many of the images shown on these pages were created.)

Police use this technique to paste different hairdos on criminals to see how the bad guys may have disguised themselves. Magazine editors can even use it to alter how a model looks by changing things like eye colour.

Most manipulated photos are harmless. But sometimes people will change images to mislead you. One university digitally erased an athlete from a game photo. This player had been dropped from the team for getting into trouble. Some wondered if the school was trying to make people forget what had happened. The picture made it seem as if the athlete had never been on the team.

# DON'T Be Fooled!

If something looks unbelievable, it probably is. Here are other clues that the picture you're looking at may not be what you think.

**Out-of-Scale Images** Ever seen a dog-size motorcycle? Doubtful. The dogs in the photo on page 75 had to be digitally adjusted to fit the bike.

**Fuzzy Outlines** "One giveaway is when some objects are fuzzy around the edges and others aren't," says digital artist Ryan Obermeyer.

**Changes in Lighting** Say a cat in the picture looks bright, but the background looks dim. That cat may have been pasted in.

**Repeating Patterns** "I was looking at a DVD cover recently," Obermeyer says. "The photo had a sidewalk made of stones, but several of the stone patterns were repeated over and over." That would not happen in real life.

**Weird Shadows** Are all the shadows going in different ways? Are some missing? Then the image is probably a fake.

Look for these clues—as well as some other silly secrets—in our roundup of funny photos that are not what they seem. At least in most of these cases, you *know* that seeing is not believing!

## VIEW LIKE A PHOTOGRAPHER
How do the photographs help readers understand the information about tricky pics?

77

## Turtle Time

One turtle? Try three turtles! "I noticed that baby turtles have the prettiest shells," says photographer Nick Vedros. "Box turtles have great legs and tails, and giant tortoises have the best faces." So Vedros combined all three to create this tricky turtle!

## Kitten Sink

Remy the cat was actually dry when his picture was taken. "We photographed the sink, the brush, and the duck separately with suds around them," photographer John Lund says.

## Something's Fishy!

Surprise! This photo is for real. "I was sport fishing with a man who brought his pet iguana," says photographer Bill Curtsinger. "The iguana climbed up the fishing pole to get a better view. It looked like he was fishing, so...." Curtsinger grabbed a camera for this real photo. It fools just about everyone.

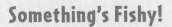

DANGER
SOFT SAND

## Big Rig

"We sat the elephant on a circus stool at a studio where cars are usually photographed," says photographer Bob Elsdale. Why? It was the only studio with a big enough door! The car is actually a toy photographed at a beach.

### DIG DEEPER

1. Choose one of the tricky pics. List the clues that tell you it is not a real picture.
2. Should the media have to tell us when they use a photo that is not real? Record your opinion. Give convincing reasons to support your view.

# Designers at Work!

Designers are often inspired by images that have a message. A poster is one way to present these types of images.

## Plan a Poster

### Choose a message.

- Brainstorm messages you might display on a poster.
- Make a web to show your ideas.

### Choose the images.

Find images that do the best job of telling your message.

- What images will catch your viewers' attention?
- Do you want images that show low angles and close-ups?

**IDEAS TO TRY**

- Think about what a poster could say about health, your community, or another topic or issue you care about.

**HINT!**

You might want to make a sketch of how the images might be placed.

### Design the layout.

- Try different ways of laying out the images.
- What do you want viewers to look at first?
- What lettering will you use for your title?

## Make the Poster

- Glue the images on the poster.
- Decide on a title for the poster. Think about how big the title will be and the colours you will use.

## Create a Poster Gallery

- Set up a class gallery of posters.
- Organize a gallery walk and invite other classes to come and view the posters you have created.

**PRESENTATION**

As you plan your poster, think about how you are using:

- colour
- lettering
- images

# MESSAGES IN STONE

by Mary Wallace

**How can you make a message that will last for years to come?**

An inuksuk (ee-nook-sook) is a stone marker that can give important information to an Arctic traveller. Three or more of these markers are called inuksuit (ee-nook-sweet). Inuksuit are found throughout the Arctic areas of Alaska, Arctic Canada, and Greenland. Inuksuit have been used by the Inuit to act in place of human messengers. For those who understand their forms, inuksuit can show direction, tell about a good hunting or fishing area, show where food is stored, indicate a good resting area, or act as a message centre.

Every inuksuk is unique because it is built from the stones at hand. An inuksuk is a strong connection to the land: it is built on the land, it is made of the land, and it tells about the land.

Here are some inuksuit. Their names are written in Inuktitut (Ee-nook-tee-toot), the language of the Inuit. Look on page 85 to learn what message each inuksuk is giving.

**VIEW LIKE AN ARTIST**

How does the artist show the beauty of the inuksuit and the vast landscape?

ᐃᓄᖕᖑᐊᒍᐊᖅ

ᓇᖅᑲᑕᐃᑦ

ᐱᐳᔅᖅᑲᔅᕕ

ᖅᑲᔅᖅᑯᐃᔅ

ᑐᐸᔅᖅᑲᒪᐅᐃᑦ

# The Messages of the Inuksuit

The Inuktitut language is written in symbols that represent a combination of sounds. Below are the names of the inuksuit shown on pages 83–84. Look at the guide to pronouncing the words. The letters in upper case show which syllable you put more emphasis on when you say the word.

| Symbol | Name | Meaning |
|---|---|---|
| ᐃᓄᐊᕐᖑᐊᖅ | **Inunnguaq** (Ee-non-WAWK) | something that resembles a person. |
| ᓇᒃᑕᑕᐃᑦ | **Nakkatait** (Nah-cut-tait) | things that fell in the water. An inuksuk with this name points to a good place to fish. |
| ᐱᕈᔭᖅᖃᕐᕕ | **Pirujaqarvik** (Pee-goo-yah-KHAK-vik) | where the meat supply is. |
| ᖃᔭᒃᑯᕕᐃᑦ | **Qajakkuviit** (Kha-yak-koo-VEET) | place for a kayak to be stored. |
| ᑐᐸᔭᖃᖕᒑᐅᑦ | **Tupjakàngaut** (Toob-jahk-hang-out) | footprints of game. This inuksuk steers hunters toward good places to hunt. |

## DIG DEEPER

1. Choose a favourite illustration from this selection. Write a journal entry telling why you like it.

2. With a partner or group, brainstorm a list of other ways people use objects to make a message. Sketch some examples.

# FROM CAVE TO

by Anne Mackenzie

**30 000– 10 000 BCE**

Cave paintings or carvings record important events.

Stories of successful hunts are painted on cave walls. Today, people are still able to "read" these messages from the past.

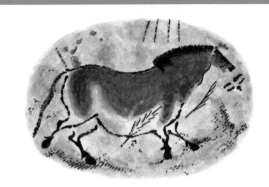

**3500–2900 BCE**

The first written languages are developed.

People in Egypt and what is now Iraq develop forms of writing made up of pictures.

**500 CE**

The first pens in Europe are made.

Some early pens, called quills, are made from goose feathers. The writer sharpens the tip and dips it into ink.

**1450s CE**

The printing press is invented in Europe.

Letters are carved backward on small blocks. The blocks can be joined to form paragraphs. They are covered with ink, then pressed on paper.

# COMPUTER

**VIEW LIKE A DESIGNER**
How do the visuals help you to understand the timeline's information?

**1752**

The first Canadian newspaper, the **Halifax Gazette**, appears.
The paper is one sheet only. News from London, Boston, and Halifax fill the page.

**1820s**

First photographs produced.
Early cameras have to be pointed at something for eight hours in order to get a photo of it.

**1842**

The first comic book appears.
"The Adventures of Obadiah Oldbuck" is North America's first graphic novel.

**1867**

The first typewriter is produced.
The first typing machine has keys like a computer. At first, the letters jam a lot. Later, the most commonly used letters are spread out across the keyboard.

87

**1927–1950s**

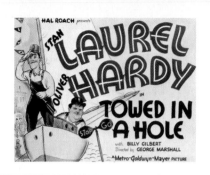

Talking motion pictures are released. Early movies are in black and white. It costs just 25 cents to watch some cartoons, see the movie, and have a drink and popcorn.

**1940s–1950s**

First TV shows for children are broadcast. At first, all shows are broadcast "live." This means the audience sees everything that happens—even the bloopers!

**1947–1951**

First electronic computer, ENIAC, is built. The ENIAC computer is as big as a house and weighs 30 tonnes. It performs calculations faster than any other machine.

**1954**

Colour TV broadcasts begin. The first RCA colour TV set costs $995. In 1954, a new car is about the same price!

**1972**

Pong starts the video game craze. *Ping, Pong.* A small dot on the screen is slowly batted back and forth. Don't miss or you lose! The graphics are simple, but people play for hours.

## Late 1970s

**Home videos become popular.**
Missed that movie at the theatre? Just rent a videocassette and watch it at home.

## 1980s

**Computer-aided graphics appear in movies.**
By the time *Jurassic Park* was made in 1993, it was getting harder and harder to tell the real thing from the special effects.

## 1990s

**Digital cameras and scanners become popular.**
People shoot and print their own pictures. Software allows images to be changed or combined. Don't believe everything you see!

## 2000 and beyond

**Smart technology lets people stay in touch.**
Cell phones allow people to make a call, send a text message, or watch TV.

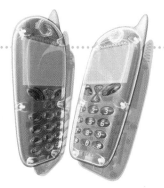

### DIG DEEPER

1. Choose two inventions that are most important to you. Give reasons for your choices.

| Most important inventions | Reasons they are important |
|---|---|
|  |  |

2. Think of a new way of communicating that has not been invented yet. Make an entry about it for the timeline. Include a sketch and a description.

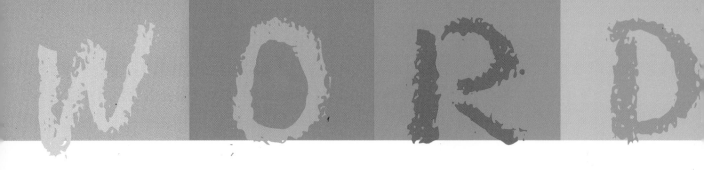

# How can letters and words send a visual message?

**S**hrin<sub>k.</sub>

h<sup>u</sup>g

snow

# STRETCH

ART

SKATEBOARD

parachute

TRIP

open
wide

Tall

**DIG DEEPER**

1. Which word art is your favourite? Explain what you like about it.

2. With a partner, create some word art of your own. Share your words with the class.

# To Each His Own

by Anna Grossnickle Hines

## How can pictures be part of a poem?

**VIEW LIKE A POET**

How do the poets create a visual message with their words?

When the leaves fall
    some float
        lazily
            wavily
and taking all
            daysily
               drift
to the ground.
Some flutter
      skuttering
           whuttering
audibly uttering
           whispers
              of sound.
When the leaves fall
    some
       come in bunches
           swirling
       and whirling
      twisting
    and twirling
        round
         about
        round.
Some
    skip-a-dip
        bippity
           floppity
             flippity
          toppity
        tippity
   plippity
      down.
And some
    just drop
      flop.

93

# giraffe

by J. Patrick Lewis
Illustrated by Lisa Desimini

Tree-tall
giraffe
up
to his
neck
in brown and yellow
patchwork quilts, turns tail
and hobbles away
on wooden
stilts stilts stilts stilts

94

# Apple

## by Cathie Peters

```
        A
         P
          P
          L
         E
     RED   RED   RED
   RED      nature's ruby      RED
    RED    plucked from a branch    RED
   RED       polished on my sleeve       RED
  RED       crisp, crunchy white flesh       RED
 RED   sometimes sweet, sometimes tart   RED
  RED        makes my tastebuds sing        RED
   RED      juice runs down my chin      RED
    RED   every bite a treat to savour   RED
     RED     the taste of summer     RED
      RED     and sunshine     RED
       RED     RED     RED
```

**DIG DEEPER** . . . . . . . . . . . . . . . . . . . . . . . . . . . . . . .

1. Choose one of the poems. Explain how the way the poem looks adds to its meaning.

2. Take turns reading one of the poems aloud with a partner. Make your voices interesting and consider adding gestures.

# ish

## by PETER H. REYNOLDS

What makes art "good" art?

Ramon loved to draw.
Anytime.
Anything.
Anywhere.

One day, Ramon was drawing
a vase of flowers.
His brother, Leon,
leaned over his shoulder.
Leon burst out laughing.
"WHAT is THAT?" he asked.

Ramon could not even answer.
He just crumpled up the drawing
and threw it across the room.

Leon's laughter haunted Ramon.
He kept trying to make his
drawings look "right,"
but they never did.

VIEW LIKE AN ARTIST
How does the art help set
the mood of the story?

After many months and
many crumpled sheets of paper,
Ramon put his pencil down.
"I'm done."

Marisol, his sister, was watching him.

"What do YOU want?" he snapped.

"I was watching you draw," she said.
Ramon sneered.
"I'm NOT drawing! Go away!"

Marisol ran away, but not before
picking up a crumpled sheet of paper.

"Hey! Come back here with that!"

Ramon raced after Marisol,
up the hall and into her room.

He was about to yell
but fell silent when
he saw his sister's walls....
He stared at the crumpled gallery.

"This is one of my favourites,"
Marisol said, pointing.

"That was SUPPOSED to be a
vase of flowers," Ramon said,
"but it doesn't look like one."

"Well, it looks vase-ISH!"
she exclaimed.

"Vase-ISH?"

Ramon looked closer.
Then he studied all the drawings on
Marisol's walls and began to
see them in a whole new way.

"They do look...ish," he said.

Ramon felt light and energized.
Thinking ish-ly allowed
his ideas to flow freely.

He began to draw what he felt—
loose lines.
Quickly springing out.
Without worry.

Ramon once again drew
and drew the world around him.
Making an ish drawing
felt wonderful.

He filled his journals...

tree-ish

house-ish

boat-ish

afternoon-ish

fish-ish

sun-ish

Ramon realized he could draw ish feelings too.

peace-ish          silly-ish          excited-ish.

His ish art inspired ish writing.
He wasn't sure if he was writing poems,
but he knew they were poem-ish.

One spring morning,
Ramon had a wonderful feeling.
It was a feeling that even ish words
and ish drawings could not capture.
He decided NOT to capture it.
Instead, he simply savoured it....

And Ramon lived ishfully ever after.

## DIG DEEPER

1. What kind of person is Marisol? Tell two
   qualities she shows in the story. Support your
   ideas with evidence from the story.

2. Create your own piece of ish art. Show it to
   three other people. Ask each of them, "What
   kind of ish do you see?"

| Marisol's qualities | Evidence |
| --- | --- |
|  |  |

# How can someone write a letter if they cannot see?

# PRIVATE AND CONFIDENTIAL

**by Marion Ripley**
**Illustrated by Colin Backhouse**

Why did the author choose to include the letters as part of the story?

"What does PRIVATE AND CONFIDENTIAL mean?" asked Laura. "There's a letter here for Mom and it's written on the envelope in big black letters."

Joe was opening his newsletter from the local football team. "It means that no one else is allowed to read it except Mom," he said. "It's probably from the bank."

"It's not fair," said Laura. "Why doesn't anyone ever write to me?"

The next day at school, Mr. Joshi made an announcement.

"I've had a letter from a teacher in Australia," he said. "If any of you would like an Australian pen pal, come and see me."

Laura was really excited. She hurried up to Mr. Joshi's classroom.

"Can I have a girl who likes swimming, gerbils, and watching television?" she asked.

"I'm sorry, Laura," said Mr. Joshi, "all the children are boys. You can have Steve, Paul, Darren, Malcolm, or Luke."

Laura was a bit disappointed. "Never mind," she said, "I'll have Malcolm."

That night Laura sat down to write her first letter to Malcolm. It was hard to know what to say.

"Just tell him about yourself and ask him to write back. That's enough to start with," said Dad.

So that's what she did.

Dear Malcolm,

I got your address from a teacher at my school. I am ten years old and go to Hollyridge School. I like swimming and watching television and talking to my friends. Sometimes I get into trouble because I talk in class and other times I'm not supposed to in assembly and supposed to!

I would really like a letter from you. please send me a photo if you can.

What is it like living in Australia?

from
Laura O'Brien

Laura waited for the post every day and it was not long before an airmail letter arrived for her—all the way from Australia!

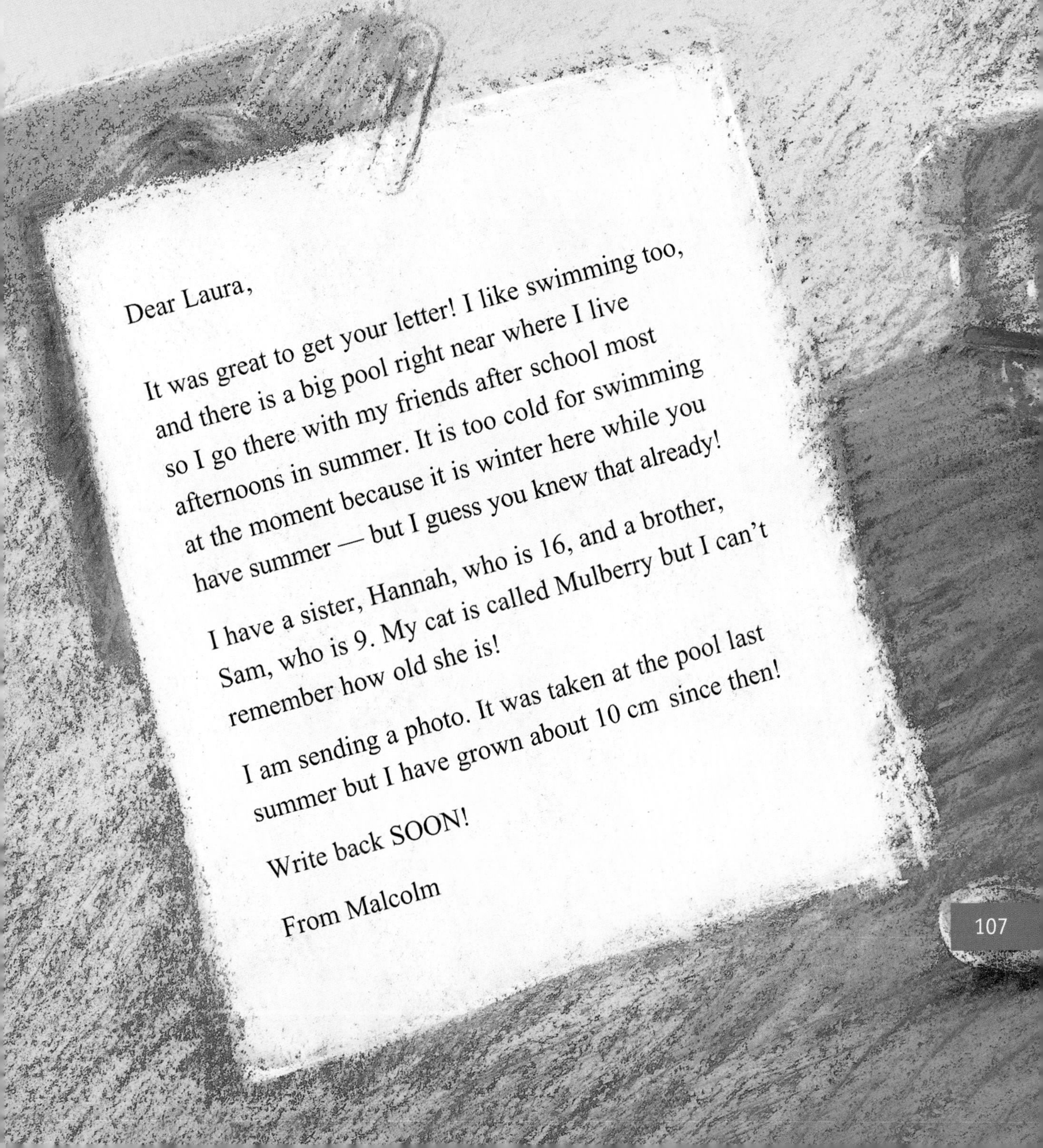

Dear Laura,

It was great to get your letter! I like swimming too, and there is a big pool right near where I live so I go there with my friends after school most afternoons in summer. It is too cold for swimming at the moment because it is winter here while you have summer — but I guess you knew that already!

I have a sister, Hannah, who is 16, and a brother, Sam, who is 9. My cat is called Mulberry but I can't remember how old she is!

I am sending a photo. It was taken at the pool last summer but I have grown about 10 cm since then!

Write back SOON!

From Malcolm

Laura really liked the letter and she really liked the photo. She took them to school and got told off for passing them round in Assembly.

That evening she wrote a long letter to Malcolm and sent him a photo even though he hadn't actually asked for one. At the end of the letter she wrote "Write back SOON!"

She posted it on her way to school the next morning.

Laura waited and waited for a reply from Malcolm, and after three weeks she still hadn't heard from him. It was really disappointing.

"Perhaps he didn't like your photo," said Joe.

At last there was a letter! But it wasn't from Malcolm.

Dear Laura,

I'm Malcolm's sister and I'm writing to you because I think you might be waiting for a letter from him.

He has had to go into hospital for an eye operation. He has very poor sight — in fact he can hardly see at all and he never will be able to. He goes to the same school as the rest of us but he types most of his work and his lesson books are in Braille.

I read your letters to him and I described your photo. He thought you sounded really nice and he has shown the photo to all his friends!

He should be out of hospital next week and I'm sure he'll write to you then.

Love from Hannah

"What's up, Laura?" asked Dad as he came into the hall.

"It's Malcolm," said Laura. "He's nearly blind. He's gone into hospital for an operation but it isn't going to make him see any better. I can't believe it. Why didn't he tell me?"

"Perhaps he didn't think it was the most important thing about him," said Dad. "Maybe he wanted to talk about swimming, and his family, and the cat instead. He was probably going to tell you when you knew each other a bit better. Does it really make that much difference?"

Laura got out the photo of Malcolm. He looked so fit and happy in the picture, it was hard to imagine him being ill in hospital. Then she had an idea. She would send him a Get Well card, and she would do it in Braille!

Karen at school had an auntie who was blind. She would probably help if she was not too busy with her baby.

After school the next day, Laura went with Karen to visit her auntie.

Karen's auntie had a brailling machine, which was a bit like a typewriter but with fewer keys. She gave Laura a Braille alphabet card and showed her how to press the keys so that they made raised dots. Then she put Laura's card in the brailler and Laura brailled her message:

Get Well Soon
Love from Laura

Ten days later a letter arrived. But it wasn't a pale blue airmail envelope this time. It was a cardboard tube with a special address label on the outside. Inside the tube was a letter—IN BRAILLE! Laura sat down on the stairs with her alphabet card to find out what it said.

"What does your letter say?" asked Joe, peering over Laura's shoulder.

"I'm not telling you," said Laura. "From now on, my letters from Malcolm are Private and Confidential!"

Here is Malcolm's braille letter. Using the alphabet card, can you find out what it says?

a b c d e f
g h i j k l m
n o p q r s
t u v w x y z

Full stop    Question mark

Exclamation mark

Here is the translation of Malcolm's letter. Did you get it right?

Dear Laura
Thank you for the card.
Can we be brailler pals instead of pen pals?
Write back soon!
Love from Malcolm

## MEDIA WATCH

Ask someone to turn on the closed captioning on a TV set. How does that change the way you view a program?

## DIG DEEPER

1. Imagine that Malcolm and Laura meet one day. With a partner, role-play what they might say to each other.

2. What would you say about yourself in a first letter to a pen pal? Write a letter to Laura in which you introduce yourself.

# Connect and Share

Almost everyone likes to get messages!

Now it's your turn to send a message.

I could bring a picture that shows how much I love my dog.

## Take a postcard home!

- Choose a selection in this unit.
- Draw one of the images from that selection.
- Show it to your family and ask them to tell you the message.
- On the back of the postcard, write the message in words.

## Bring a postcard back!

- Ask family members to help you choose a photo or make a picture that tells something about you.
- Work together to write a caption to describe it.
- Display the postcards in the classroom.

### WRITING A CAPTION

- Don't write too much.
- Tell the key message of the image.
- Print neatly so everyone can read it.

# Spotlight on **Learning**

## Collect

- Gather your notebooks, poster, and other work you did in this unit.

## Talk and reflect

Work with a partner.

- Together, read the Learning Goals on page 56.
- Talk about how well you met these goals.
- Look through your work for evidence.

## Select

- Choose two pieces of work that show how you achieved the Learning Goals. (The same piece of work can show more than one goal.)

## Tell about your choices

- Tell what each piece shows about your learning.

| My choices | I want this in my portfolio because... |
|---|---|
|  |  |

## Reflect

- What have you learned about how to view and create visual messages?
- What have you discovered about what makes a photograph interesting?
- What have you learned about how interesting illustrations or layouts can add to a story or poem?

115

# Survivors!

## LEARNING GOALS

In this unit you will:

- Read and listen to non-fiction and fiction texts about plants and animals in different habitats.

- Explain how nature and people can affect habitats.

- Use science words to describe different habitats.

- Investigate and share information about a habitat using diagrams, illustrations, and headings.

habitat
camouflage
species
endangered
wildlife
environment
conservation
food chains

117

# HOPPING

Gabrielle Félio holds one of the Petrie Island bullfrogs.

# :o the Rescue
by Sydney Grant

How can people show they care about saving habitats?

## Close Call

When the snow started to fall last December in southern Ontario, the frogs of Petrie Island Pond were already hibernating. But they almost didn't get the chance. Only days before truckloads of sand were scheduled to fill in the frogs' pond, the Amphibian Conservation Club (ACC) came to their rescue.

The summer before, kids in the ACC learned that the pond on Petrie Island, in the Ottawa River, was destined to become a parking lot. They set to work learning everything they could about the pond, especially the wildlife that lived there.

They discovered leopard frogs, green frogs, bullfrogs, mink frogs, snapping turtles, painted turtles, and so much more—and knew that they couldn't leave them to be buried by asphalt.

## Moving Day

That summer they started catching tadpoles and frogs and moved them to their new home, another pond about one kilometre away. By November, time was running out.

Petrie Island is in the Ottawa River, just north and east of Ottawa.

119

ACC members safely carry frogs to their new habitat in carrying cases.

Saturday, November 22, was their last chance. Members of the ACC leapt into action, catching frogs in nets and helping them make their trip to their new pond. The city donated two water pumps to suck the water out of the pond and into the river. Anything small enough to travel with the water got a fast water-tube ride.

As the water in the pond went down lower and lower, ACC kids just kept catching frogs. Even though it was cold, the frogs had plenty of energy to try to outrun the kids working to save them. The muck was so thick, 12-year-old ACC leader Gabrielle Félio got stuck in the mud up to her knees and needed some saving of her own!

In total, they moved 145 frogs; countless tadpoles, fish, and insects; one turtle; and a muskrat.

ACC members share information about Petrie Island's wildlife.

## In the Spotlight

It was a moving day nobody would forget, and news of the ACC spread. Run by kids, for kids, the ACC is definitely different. Gabrielle started it two years ago.

She never imagined the club would become so popular. She found herself interested in frogs after her family built a pond in their backyard. Gabrielle wanted to learn more about pond life and went looking for other kids who wanted to join in the fun.

The club began meeting at the local community centre. They would get together to do activities, arts, and crafts and to learn more about wildlife in ponds and the environment they need to live. There are now about 30 kids in the club, and meetings are held every two months at the centre—no adults allowed!

Gabrielle holds one of her awards.

## Great Rewards

Gabrielle and the ACC received a Canadian Wildlife Federation Youth Conservation Award for their fab froggy feats. Gabrielle has also been awarded an Orléans Online Outstanding Youth Award and an Arbour Environmental Foundation Youth Award. For Gabrielle, however, the biggest and best reward is seeing frogs where they belong.

### LET'S TALK ABOUT IT

- With a partner, think of some questions you would ask Gabrielle in an interview.

- What could you and others your age do to care for the environment where you live?

# Reading in Science

Reading in science helps you learn true facts and information about the world we live in. Think about a science book or TV program you've enjoyed.

- What was it about?
- How did it capture your interest?
- How was it different from reading or viewing a story?

## TALK ABOUT IT!

- Tell a partner something you learned from the book or program.
- Talk about the different places you can find science information.

  Here are some clues.

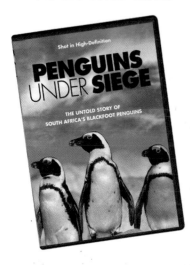

Make a chart together.

| Science Information | |
|---|---|
| Where you can find it | Examples |
| | |

# Think Like a Reader

## Read with a purpose

- Why do you read about science topics?

*scientist – science*
*naturalist – nature*
*conservation –*
*endangered –*

## Crack the code

When you see technical and difficult words in science, look for parts of the word you know.

## Make meaning

Practise using these strategies when you are reading in science:

| | |
|---|---|
| **ASK QUESTIONS** | Look at all the information in the text and visuals. Think about what you know about the topic. Ask questions about what you would like to know. |
| **PAUSE AND CHECK** | Pause at the end of each paragraph or section to check your understanding. |
| **SUMMARIZE** | Organize the information in a chart or web. |

## Analyze what you read

- How can you find "true" information about a science topic?
- Why might there be different points of view about a science topic?

# Life in a Pond

# Frogs

ASK
QUESTIONS

What would you like
to know about a
frog's habitat?

The Northern Leopard Frog is found in all provinces of
Canada.

Long before the dinosaurs, frogs lived on earth.
They belong to the amphibian family. Amphibians
can live in water and on land.

There are more than 4000 kinds of frogs in the
world. In Canada, there are 21 kinds.

## Appearance

Most frogs in Canada are green, grey, or brown.

Frogs have smooth wet skin. They have long
back legs to help them jump. Their webbed feet
help them swim. Frogs' eyes bulge out from the
sides of their heads. This helps them see from
behind.

The bodies of most frogs are 5 to 10 cm long.
Some frogs can be as long as 30 cm.

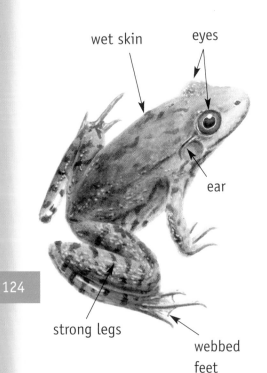

wet skin

eyes

ear

strong legs

webbed
feet

124

## Food

Frogs eat insects, caterpillars, and earthworms. Larger frogs will even eat mice and fish. Frogs do not hunt for food but sit quietly and wait until their prey comes near. Then the frog catches its prey with its long sticky tongue.

A frog has teeth in its top jaw only. So a frog swallows its prey without chewing it.

The Pacific Tree Frog lives in British Columbia. It has sticky pads on its toes that help it climb.

## Habitat

Frogs live close to water. Most live in ponds or swamps, or near a lake. Some frogs live in trees. In cold places, frogs hibernate in winter.

Frogs lay their eggs in water. The eggs hatch into tadpoles that live in the water until they become adult frogs. Then they move onto land.

In many parts of Canada, frogs are losing their habitat. Builders clear the land to build houses and roads. Frogs have no place to live.

**PAUSE AND CHECK**

What have you learned about frogs so far? Does it make sense?

Adult frog: The tail has been reabsorbed by the body.

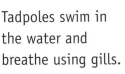

rog eggs are aid in water.

**Frog Life Cycle**

The froglet still has some of its tail but breathes using lungs.

Tadpoles swim in the water and breathe using gills.

Tadpole with legs.

125

**SUMMARIZE**

How can you organize the information in a chart or web?

# Life in the Arctic
# Polar Bears

Female polar bears usually give birth to twins.

## ASK QUESTIONS
What would you like to know about a polar bear's habitat?

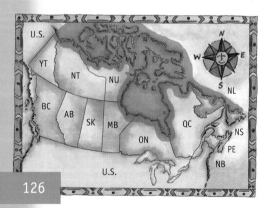

The area in dark blue shows where polar bears can be found in Canada.

About 15 000 polar bears live in Canada's Arctic.

The polar bear is a mammal. It is also the largest bear in the world. The polar bear is different from other bears because it does not hibernate.

## Appearance

The polar bear's fur appears white. But in fact each hair is transparent—just like the colour of water. Under its fur, the polar bear's skin is black.

An adult male polar bear weighs from 350 to 650 kg. When standing, he can measure up to 3 m tall. Female polar bears weigh 150 to 250 kg. Newborn polar bears weigh less than half a kg.

back legs are shorter than front legs

small, rounded ears

black eyes

large paws

126

## Food

The polar bear is called a carnivore because it eats meat. Its favourite food is the ringed seal. To hunt its prey, the polar bear waits patiently by the seal's hole in the ice, until the seal comes up for air. Then the polar bear grabs it.

Polar bears do not drink water. They get all the water they need from the animals they eat.

**PAUSE AND CHECK**

What have you learned about polar bears so far? Does it make sense?

## Habitat

The polar bear's habitat is in and around the Arctic Ocean. In winter, when it is very cold, the polar bear's fur and black skin help to keep it warm.

Polar bears travel about 24 km a day looking for food. They swim, or walk over large chunks of floating ice.

The climate of Earth is getting warmer, causing the ice in the polar bears' habitat to slowly melt. Because this habitat is slowly disappearing, scientists think that polar bears may no longer exist in a hundred years.

**SUMMARIZE**

How can you organize the information in a chart or web?

Polar bears are very strong swimmers.

127

# Life in an Ocean

# Blue Whales

The head of the blue whale forms up to a quarter of its total body length.

Blue whales live in the ocean. They are the largest mammals on Earth, and they are also the loudest! They make sounds that are louder than those of a jet plane.

There are only about 3000 blue whales left in the world today. Blue whales are often called "blues."

**ASK QUESTIONS**

What would you like to know about a blue whale's habitat?

## Appearance

A blue whale is actually blue-grey in colour with lighter spots. Blues have two tail flukes that measure about 7.5 m from tip to tip. The blue's nostrils are the blowholes on the top of its head.

A female blue whale can measure up to 30 m in length and weigh 130 000 kg. Male blues are smaller.

dorsal fin

flukes

2 blowholes

baleen plates in mouth

flippers →

## Food

A blue whale needs to eat from 900 to 4100 kg of krill a day. Krill are small creatures like shrimp. When feeding, the blue takes in an enormous gulp of water and closes its mouth. Krill get trapped in its baleen as the whale forces the water out. Baleen are the whale's teeth and they look like large combs.

Under their skin, blues have a layer of fat called blubber. In winter, they do not eat for months, but live off their own blubber.

## Habitat

Blues are found in oceans all over the world except in the far north. About 100 blues live in Canada's Gulf of St. Lawrence.

In spring and summer, blues like cool water where there is plenty of krill. In the winter, they migrate to warmer waters where their calves are born.

Blue whales have been an endangered species since 1966. In the past, whalers hunted blue whales for their oil, meat, and bones. Today, the main threats to their ocean habitat are oil spills and pollution.

Scientists can identify a blue whale by its flukes. This helps them keep track of how many whales are in an area.

**PAUSE AND CHECK**
What have you learned about blue whales so far? Does it make sense?

Krill are an important food for many fish and other animals that live in the sea.

**SUMMARIZE**
How can you organize the information in a chart or web?

# Reflect on Your Reading

**You have . . .**

- talked about animal habitats.
- read about different animal habitats.
- learned new vocabulary that tells about animal habitats.

amphibian
carnivore
hibernate
mammal
environment
prey

*I think some animal habitats are being destroyed and it's hard for the animals to survive. What do you think?*

**You have also . . .**

- explored different reading strategies.

**ASK QUESTIONS**

**PAUSE AND CHECK**

**SUMMARIZE**

## Write About Learning

Write about one of the strategies you used when you read the selection "Animal Habitats." How did the strategy help you read and understand the selection? Tell how the strategy might help you when you read other explanations in science.

# Read Like a Writer

When you were reading "Animal Habitats," you were reading some *explanations*. An explanation describes what something is like or how something works.

## TALK ABOUT IT!

- What do you notice about the way explanations are written?
  Make a chart to list what you know about explanations.

**HINT!**
What do you notice about the **ideas** and **details** the author uses?

Explanations

- have a title that gives the topic
- give details so readers can understand
- have pictures or diagrams to add details

# Canadian Habitat

## by Trudee Romanek

How can ordinary people help save habitats?

Mairuth Sarsfield

### For Every Child a Tree

In 1972, many countries took part in an important conference. They vowed to take care of our planet. Ten years later, though, things were no better. More forests had been cut down. Deserts were getting bigger. Mairuth Sarsfield wanted to remind countries of the vow they had made. She worked for the United Nations Environment Programme.

Mairuth suggested countries replace the trees they had cut down. She wanted children to plant the new seedlings. She thought that might help them to feel connected to nature and want to take care of it. Her team organized an event called "For Every Child a Tree."

Fourteen countries agreed to take part. Some donated extra trees for countries that couldn't afford to buy their own. Mairuth's efforts made a difference. Children planted more than 3 billion seedlings all over the world.

Mairuth knew deserts were getting bigger, especially in Asia and Africa.

# Heroes

**READ LIKE A WRITER**

What facts and details did the author include to keep you reading?

## Turtle Champion

Mike James knows a lot about leatherback turtles. He knows that some of them weigh over 450 kg. He knows that they hatch on a beach and crawl to the water. From then on, they spend most of their lives swimming. Many of these turtles swim from the warm waters of the Caribbean all the way up to the coast of Nova Scotia. Mike knows that along the way they sometimes swim into danger.

Leatherback turtles breathe air, just like people do. They rise up and poke their heads above the water to breathe. If a turtle gets caught in a fishing net, sometimes it can't get to the water's surface. Then the turtle will drown. Mike James and his team at the Nova Scotia Leatherback Turtle Working Group want to make sure that doesn't happen.

So far, Mike's team has taught 500 volunteers how to free leatherback turtles caught in nets. Together, they are making the Nova Scotia habitat safer for the turtles.

Mike James

This leatherback turtle is laying her eggs in the sand.

133

The Jefferson salamander is one species that Natalie works to protect.

Natalie Helferty

# Pathfinder

Wild animals travel a lot. Some migrate for winter. Others move around to find food. When people build a city, or even a single road, it sometimes blocks animals from getting where they need to go.

The ever-growing cities and towns in southern Ontario make it hard for animals to get from one patch of wilderness to another. So, Natalie Helferty has tried to keep some pathways open.

Natalie is a biologist. She lives on a long ridge of land called the Oak Ridges Moraine. In this moraine there are towns and cities as well as woods, lakes, bogs, and other animal habitats. Many frogs, salamanders, turtles, snakes, and even deer and foxes live there.

Natalie helps developers plan before they build so that the wilderness pathways do not get blocked. She also suggests new pathways be made to help animals avoid roads already in their way. Because of her work, local governments have built tunnels under roadways. Natalie has even suggested a special wildlife bridge for large animals like deer and coyotes.

Natalie believes that, in most cases, animals just need people to stay out of their way. If we do that, we may get to keep these wild creatures as neighbours.

# Friend of the Arctic

Andy Carpenter has spent his whole life in Arctic Canada. The land and its creatures are very important to him. Andy is a very skillful hunter and trapper, but he follows the code of the Inuvialuit people. He takes only as many animals as his family needs.

Andy Carpenter

Andy noticed that oil companies had started to explore and drill in the Arctic. He also noticed that more hunters were coming north. He worried that these changes might not be good for the land. So Andy decided to make sure the people of the Arctic would have animals to hunt in the future.

Andy helped to establish Aulavik National Park, home to a large group of muskoxen and the endangered Peary caribou. He also helped to create Ivvavik National Park. Then Andy and his people joined with other Arctic groups to create an action plan to protect polar bears.

Muskoxen

Andy Carpenter has worked hard to do what's right for Arctic Canada. That way, he hopes, the animals he respects will always be there.

## DIG DEEPER

1. Make a three-column chart to summarize what you learned about each habitat hero.

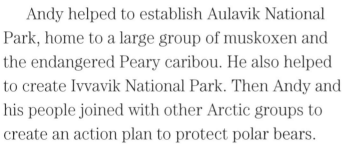

| Hero | Problem | Solution |
|------|---------|----------|
|      |         |          |

2. Create a sign or slogan for a habitat that is at risk.

MEDIA WATCH

Look for stories about other habitat heroes in newspapers and magazines.

# Food Chains
## by Peter Riley

## How are food chains and habitats closely connected?

**READ LIKE A WRITER**
What visual features in the text help you to understand food chains?

The way plants and animals are linked together by feeding is called a food chain. Most food chains start with energy from the sun. Plants use this energy to grow. In turn, the plants may be eaten by animals, and these animals by other animals.

# Grasslands

The grasslands of North America, Africa, and Australia each have their own unique food chains.

## North America

The meadows of North America and Europe are home to field mice. These animals eat the lower part of grass stems. Field mice make tunnels through the grass to hide from predators like hawks and owls. A predator is an animal that kills and eats other animals.

On the plains, prairie dogs make burrows in which to hide from predators such as coyotes and hawks. They eat the grass around their home so they can see any approaching attackers.

sun

grass          prairie dog          hawk

In this food chain, the grass uses energy from the sun to grow. The prairie dog eats the grass, then the hawk feeds on the prairie dog.

Black-tailed prairie dog. In Canada, they are found only in southern Saskatchewan.

## The African Plains

Large numbers of zebras, gnus, and Thomson's gazelles graze on the African plains. Zebras eat the tops of the grass first, then gnus eat the middle part of the grass. Thomson's gazelles eat the young shoots that are left behind. All these animals are herbivores, which means they eat only plants. They may become prey to lions, hyenas, and other carnivores.

## The Australian Outback

In Australia, grasses are eaten by kangaroos and wallabies. These herbivores may be eaten by packs of wild dogs called dingoes. Grass seeds are eaten by diamond firetail finches, which in turn are eaten by the peregrine falcon. The falcon dives out of the sky to attack and feed on the finches.

The diamond firetail finch is found in the wild only in Australia.

You can tell the age of a tree by counting its rings.

# Woodlands

There are woodlands in many parts of the world. The trees store food in the wood they make, and carry water from their roots to their leaves in tiny pipelines in their trunks and branches.

## Tree Rings

The pipelines make rings in the wood every year. When the weather is good, the tree makes a large amount of food and grows a wide ring. When the weather is poor, the tree makes a narrow ring.

## Woodland Insects

Bark beetles burrow underneath the bark, feeding on the rings of wood. Woodpeckers prey on bark beetles, striking the wood with their chisel-shaped beaks. They use their long tongues to lick the beetles out of their burrows.

A pileated woodpecker

Some spiders spin webs between twigs. They hide on a twig, waiting for an insect to fly into the web and become stuck on its threads. As the insect struggles, the spider rushes up to it and gives it a poisonous bite.

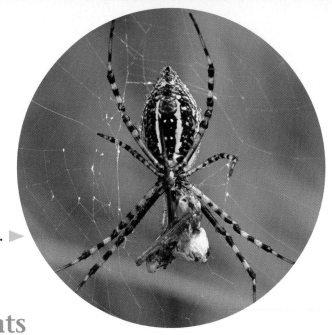

This orb weaver spider has trapped prey in its web. ▶

Each gypsy moth caterpillar can eat an average of one square metre of leaves. This can damage or kill a tree.

## Bats

Moth caterpillars feed on leaves. They are camouflaged, so many of them escape predators. When they become moths, they fly at night, trying to avoid bats. These predators roost in tree holes during the day and fly through the woodland at night, feeding on moths and other insects such as gnats and beetles.

## Woodland Birds

The tree creeper bird feeds on insects and spiders, using its hooked beak to pull them out of their hiding places.

This tree creeper bird is found throughout southern Canada, but its camouflage makes it difficult to spot.

A thirsty camel can drink up to 100 litres in 10 minutes.

# Desert

All life needs water. In a desert it may rain for only a very short time in a year, so the plants here have adapted to survive. Their long roots collect as much water from the ground as possible.

## Surviving Without Rain

Since plants lose water through their leaves, desert plants have only small leaves. Some plants have only spines. Some plants survive the dry conditions by remaining as seeds while it is dry. When it rains, they germinate and grow quickly into plants.

Desert plants have long roots and small leaves or spines.

Desert animals are also able to survive without much water. One of the best known, the camel, lives in the Sahara Desert. It can manage for weeks without drinking any water—as long as it can find succulent desert plants to eat. These are plants that store water in their leaves and stems.

Swarms of locusts can devour a plant's leaves in a matter of seconds.

## Desert Plants and Food Chains

Because of their stores of water, desert plants provide the basis for many desert food chains. Insects that eat desert plants include locusts, grasshoppers, and crickets. These animals, in turn, provide food for lizards, birds, and scorpions.

A scorpion

In cold deserts, lichen and moss grow on rocks and on the ground. Here, an Arctic tern chick nestles between lichen-covered rocks.

### DIG DEEPER

1. How is a food chain affected when the habitat is changed by lack of rain?
2. Investigate a food chain in a rainforest, pond, or on a mountain. Draw a diagram to explain your food chain and habitat.

141

# Researchers at Work!

Scientists investigate topics that interest them. They share what they find out in different ways.

A brochure is one way to explain what you have learned, so that others can learn about the topic too.

## Choose a Habitat to Research

- Think about the animal and plant habitats you have read about.
- What question about habitats would you like to explore?
- Brainstorm ideas with a partner or in a group.

## Plan Your Research

- Choose a research question.
- List different resources you can use to help you find the answer.
- Decide how you will record the information.

### RESEARCH TIPS

- Look for information in books, magazines, and on CD-ROMs.
- Browse Web sites, like the site for the Canadian Wildlife Federation.
- Interview an expert about your habitat.
- View science videos and TV programs.

# Create a Brochure

Make a brochure to share what you learned.

Here are some important things to think about:

- your audience
- how you will organize the information
- what you will put on the front of the brochure
- what visuals you will use
- how you will make the brochure

# Display the Brochure

- Think of how you can share your brochure in different ways.
- You could place the brochure in the library resource centre or create a classroom display.

## PRESENTATION POINTERS

- Is the information presented clearly?
- Did you include science vocabulary?
- Did you use a variety of text and design features?
- Will the reader learn something about the topic?

# ART Underfoot

by Jeff Siamon

How can art help people think about the natural world?

Drain covers usually look something like this.

The city of Vancouver uses art to remind people to care about the environment. Recently, the city held a competition called Art Underfoot. The winning designs in the competition will be cast in iron on city drain covers. If you've noticed drain covers before, they are usually round, made of metal, and cover the openings to underground sewers. Drain covers are usually grimy and dirty—*not* works of art.

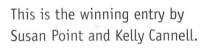

This is the winning entry by Susan Point and Kelly Cannell.

One of the winning designs was by the team of Susan Point and Kelly Cannell. Susan and Kelly are from the Musqueam First Nation in Vancouver. They are also mother and daughter. Much of their work is based on traditional Coast Salish art and designs.

Their drain cover shows the life cycle of a frog. The design will remind people to not put harmful chemicals down their drains. When people dump chemicals, they can travel to the bodies of water where frogs live and breed.

You can also see that the winning design forms a circle of images. The eggs in the centre swirl out into tadpoles, then into frogs. Susan Point often presents images in a circle pattern. This helps viewers understand that all things in nature are somehow connected, with no end and no beginning, just like a circle.

So, the next time you are out for a walk, look down at your feet. You might see something that is both beautiful *and* makes you think!

**READ LIKE A WRITER**
How do details in the artwork tell about the natural world?

Kelly Cannell (left) and Susan Point are Coast Salish artists. They have also worked together on silkscreen prints, paintings, and wood carvings.

## DIG DEEPER

1. In what ways could the water that goes down a drain hurt a habitat?

2. Design a drain cover that will remind people to respect the environment.

# Friends of the
# BLUE PLANET

## How Children Feel About Our Environment

Poppy Edmunds (age 9) England

## How can children share ideas about our planet?

Dear Friends of the Blue Planet,

When I am in the middle of nature I feel that it is part of my family. If any child breaks a branch off a tree, I feel sorrow, as if they had broken a part of my soul.

If every leaf, every blade of grass, every tree, every flower were to disappear, I would feel like I was losing my family.

Your friend,
Lurubaru Mihaela (age 12)
Romania

Erickson Joseph (age 10)
Dominica

Without
Our
Respect
  our
Land
  will be
Destroyed

Your friend,
Megan O'Keeffe (age 12)
Australia

**READ LIKE A WRITER**
Why did the children use "feelings" words and phrases to express their views about the environment?

My favourite part of nature is to be with the Sisserou parrots. I would like to play and talk with the Sisserou, and help them make a huge family so that they may show the world that they are special.

My dream is that man may not destroy everything of Dominica but will see the wonders and I want this dream to come true. My children in time to come will continue my dream. And they will do the same thing that I did.

Ricard St. John (age 10)
Dominica

I am happy to see the trees. The trees give us medicines. If you cut the trees down the dryness will come. When you cut the trees down the rain carries the topsoil away. In my opinion, if there are no trees everyone will die.

Badra Plea (age 13)
Mali

Dear World,

I live in the country and most of the trees are dead. You can take a walk through there and some of the trees, if you touch them, they may fall or break. A lot of it is the acid rain. There is a creek there and the deer drink that water. The water is orange and it is mainly from acid rain.

Your friend,
Jennifer Stroud (age 10)
Canada

Don't cut my house.

STOP! Don't cut me, I am you friend.

I will cut this tree because my master told me to.

STOP! You can't cut this tree because it is useful to us.

Sandeep Yadava (age 9)
India

148

Eri Kitakubo (age 11)
Japan

My Friends,

I dream that people will not throw everything into the environment, and that people will understand that they are only harming themselves. One can only hope.

Stefan Wieland (age 9)
Germany

Dear people all over the globe!

I want all the people on earth to gather as one united family and clear nature of pollution. Also I want every person on earth to do some good deed for the preservation of nature! Take care of nature!

Marina Semyonova (age 10)
Russia

## DIG DEEPER

1. Choose your favourite letter or poem. What would you say to the author about their work?

2. Create your own letter, poem, or drawing to show how you feel about the environment.

149

# How Does a Possum Cross the Road?

## by Andrew Charman

**READ LIKE A WRITER**

Why do you think the author chose Question and Answer format?

**Why are some animals survivors and others endangered?**

### Q How does a possum cross the road?

**A** Today the rare mountain pygmy possums of Australia use an underpass! When a road was built through their reserve, many males were hit by cars when they went to visit the females. A tunnel was built for them to cross the road safely.

For many years, people thought mountain pygmy possums were extinct. Then, in 1966, a live possum was discovered.

### Q Which endangered animal is the most shy?

**A** The shy okapi is so hard to find that scientists didn't even know it existed until 1901. Today there are fewer okapis than ever, because their rain forest home is being cut down.

It looks much like a zebra, but the okapi is actually a relative of the giraffe.

## Why are boats bad for manatees?

**A** Manatees are gentle animals—they spend their life swimming along, grazing on sea grass. Unfortunately, they share their waterways with fast-moving boats, and many manatees are injured by propeller blades. This means the animals are getting rarer.

| Manatees killed in Florida by watercraft KEY: = 10 manatees | |
|---|---|
| 1975 | 6 |
| 1985 | 33 |
| 1995 | 42 |
| 2005 | 80 |

The largest population of manatees is found in Florida.

## Which "extinct" animal returned to the wild?

**A** Père David's deer were once extinct in the wild. The only ones left lived in zoos and parks. Luckily they were bred so successfully that now they are being returned to their grassland homes in northern China.

Adult deer have summer coats that are bright red with a dark stripe. They have dark grey coats in winter.

## Which fox flies to its food?

**A** The Rodrigues flying fox isn't a fox—it's a bat that lives on Rodrigues Island. It eats fruit, so it needs lots of fruit trees. Sadly, most of its forest home has been cut down and there are now only about 400 of these bats left.

The body of the Rodrigues flying fox is quite small, but its wing span can be up to 90 cm across.

Rodrigues Island is in the Indian Ocean, about 550 km northeast of the island of Mauritius.

## Which endangered whale has a unicorn's horn?

**A** The narwhal is a kind of whale that lives in the Arctic seas. The male is hunted for its spiralled tusk, which looks just like a unicorn's horn. If too many narwhals are taken, they may one day become extinct.

The tusk is really a narwhal's left tooth that has grown outward in a spiral. Narwhal tusks can grow to be 2 to 3 m long.

# Q  Who grabs robber crabs?

**A**  Robber crabs live on islands in the Pacific and Indian Oceans. Some grow up to nearly a metre across. They are hunted for food and made into souvenirs for tourists.

Robber crabs climb trees, such as coconut trees, and snip off fruit with their giant pincers. They then climb down the tree, gather the fruit, and pound it until they get it open to eat.

## MEDIA WATCH

Look for stories about endangered animals or habitats.

## DIG DEEPER

1. How can endangered animals and their habitats be brought to people's attention? Discuss with a partner some ways to raise people's awareness of habitat loss.

2. Locate some interesting facts about an endangered animal habitat. Create your own Question and Answer card to share the information with others.

# Dare to Care...

Sponsored by the Canadian Association of Principals, Canadian Museum of Nature, Canadian Wildlife Federation, Coastal Zone Canada Association, Environment Canada (Biodiversity Convention Office and Marine Environment Branch), Fisheries and Oceans Canada, Parks Canada, and Scouts Canada.

154

How can a poster create
interest in a natural habitat?

# Special Marine Places...Get to Know One

Celebrate Oceans Day June 8

## DIG DEEPER

1. What can you learn about this natural habitat by looking closely at the images and words?

2. In a small group, brainstorm some different ways that Oceans Day could be promoted across Canada.

156

**READ LIKE A WRITER**
What kinds of words does the author use to paint a vivid picture in your mind of this underwater habitat?

# Sea Otter Inlet
### by Celia Godkin

How can people affect habitats in both positive and negative ways?

In a long arm of the sea,
hemmed in by land on either side,
lived a colony of sea otters.

The sea otters lived their whole lives
in the waters of this inlet.
They dived in the deep
seaweedy forests of kelp,
looking for good things to eat.
They dined on crabs and shellfish,
on sea stars and octopi,
but their favourite food of all
was the spiny purple sea urchin.

After a meal of these delicacies,
the otters groomed themselves with great care.
When they were as clean as they could be,
they wrapped themselves in a frond of kelp
and went to sleep.
The kelp anchored them gently in place
so they could not drift away.

One day the otters awoke from their nap
to find hunters all around.
The hunters hurled harpoons at them
or shot them with guns.

The otters dived to escape the hunters.
But they could not stay below the water for ever.
The hunters waited patiently
for the otters to come up for air.

One by one,
the otters were hunted and killed
for their soft, warm fur.
When there were no more otters left,
the hunters sailed away,
and life in the kelp forest went on.

There were clingfish
clinging to the flat, leaf-like blades of the kelp.
There were kelpfish eating the clingfish.
There were sea bass eating the kelpfish.
And there were many more fishes,
too numerous to mention,
swimming in and out of the kelp forest.

The kelp forest was made of giant seaweeds
with flat leaf-like blades
attached to a long, flexible stem.
The stem went way way down
into the watery depths
and attached at the bottom
to a firm piece of rock.
The attachment—called a holdfast—
anchored the kelp plant
so it would not float away.

Living on the bottom,
on and around the kelp holdfasts,
were all kinds of shellfish.
Some lived in cupped shells.
Some lived in coiled shells, like snails.
And some lived in shells
made of two halves hinged together.

There were flower-like sea anemones.
There were crabs and lobsters and shrimps.
There were eight-legged octopi,
and many-legged sun stars,
and five-legged sea stars and brittle stars,
and there were spiny purple sea urchins
with no legs at all.

For a long, long time,
life in the kelp forest went on
much as it always had done.
Except that there were no sea otters
collecting crabs and shellfish,
or sea stars and octopi,
and there were no sea otters
collecting their favourite food;
the spiny purple sea urchin.

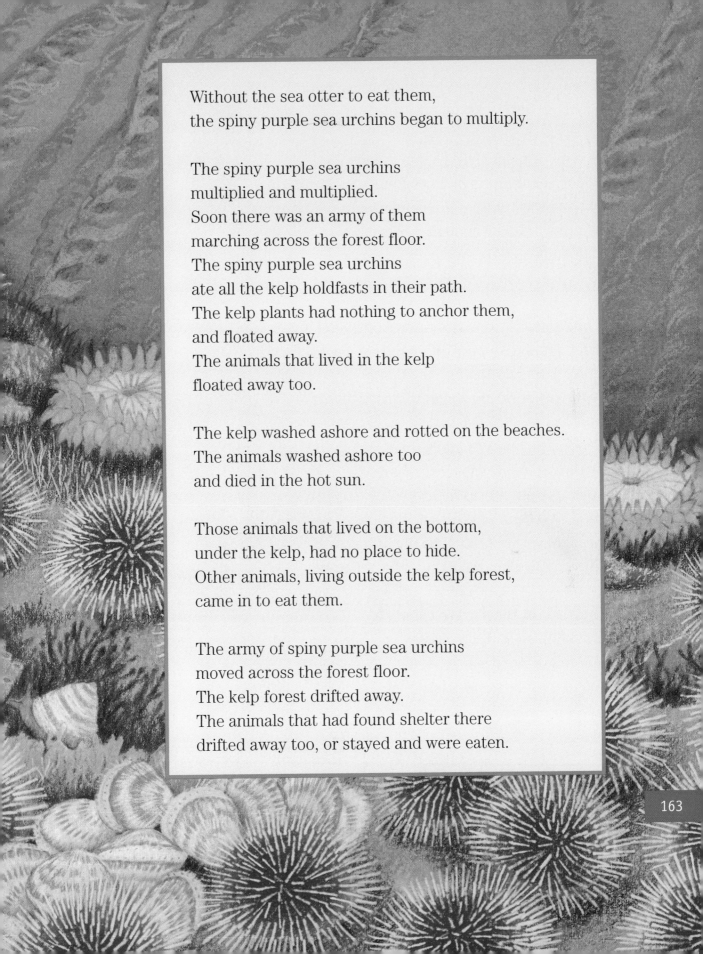

Without the sea otter to eat them,
the spiny purple sea urchins began to multiply.

The spiny purple sea urchins
multiplied and multiplied.
Soon there was an army of them
marching across the forest floor.
The spiny purple sea urchins
ate all the kelp holdfasts in their path.
The kelp plants had nothing to anchor them,
and floated away.
The animals that lived in the kelp
floated away too.

The kelp washed ashore and rotted on the beaches.
The animals washed ashore too
and died in the hot sun.

Those animals that lived on the bottom,
under the kelp, had no place to hide.
Other animals, living outside the kelp forest,
came in to eat them.

The army of spiny purple sea urchins
moved across the forest floor.
The kelp forest drifted away.
The animals that had found shelter there
drifted away too, or stayed and were eaten.

Then, one day, a wonderful thing happened.
Some sea otters swam into the inlet.

Some otters had survived in places
which the hunters had not found.
No one was hunting them anymore.
There were now enough otters
that some could come back
to live again in their old home.

The otters dived in the waters of the inlet.
They found plenty of spiny purple sea urchins.
Their favourite food!
Soon, other otters joined them.

Gradually, very gradually,
as the otters ate more and more
spiny purple sea urchins,
the kelp began to grow back again.
Gradually, very gradually, the animals
that had lived in the kelp forest returned.

Once again, there were clingfish
and kelpfish and sea bass,
and many more fishes,
too numerous to mention.

There were all kinds of shellfish.
There were flower-like sea anemones,
and crabs and lobsters and shrimps.
There were eight-legged octopi
and many-legged sun stars
and five-legged sea stars and brittle stars.

There were even
some spiny purple sea urchins,
with no legs at all.
But not too many.

## DIG DEEPER

1. How did people change this natural habitat?
2. In a small group, choose two or three parts of this story for choral reading. Practise reading the selection before performing for an audience.

How should the natural habitats
of our world be preserved?

# Solomon's Tree

## by ANDREA SPALDING
## Illustrated by JANET WILSON

The cedar trees around Solomon's house were special. They shaded in summer and sheltered in winter and whispered secrets to each other on the breath of the wind.

But the big old maple was very special. This was the tree that shared its secrets with Solomon. Every day Solomon climbed its knobby trunk and curled up in his favourite notch.

"Hello, tree," he whispered and stroked the rough bark.

"Hello, Solomon," the tree rustled back. Its branches cradled his body.

In spring the maple showed him a hummingbird nest. Solomon gazed in astonishment at the fragment of woven lichen clinging to a forked twig and marvelled at the tiny eggs, smaller than his little fingernail.

"You mustn't tell," whispered the tree.

"I promise," Solomon whispered back.

In summer the maple showed Solomon where the chrysalis hung, hidden in a crack of bark.

"Watch carefully," whispered the tree.

"I will," Solomon whispered back.

He watched with wonder as the chrysalis cracked open, and bit by bit a brand-new butterfly unfolded its wings and danced away on the breeze.

**READ LIKE A WRITER**

The author uses the senses (sight, touch, smell, sound, taste) to show Solomon's relationship to the tree. How does this help the reader understand how he feels?

167

In fall the maple shed its golden leaves and winged seeds and rustled and chuckled as it showered Solomon. Solomon chased the dancing propellers and gathered together piles of leaves.

"Winter's coming," whispered the tree.

"I know," Solomon answered softly from under his leafy blanket.

With the winter came wind and rain. The cedars surrounding Solomon's house tossed their branches and chanted winter songs. The big old maple creaked out lullabies to comfort Solomon's sleep.

Then came a midwinter storm. The wind howled and shrieked. Inside Solomon's house only the voice of the wind could be heard.

"This storm is too big," said Solomon. "I'm scared." He burrowed under his quilt and pulled the pillow around his ears.

The storm raged for hours, whipping the treetops back and forth and playing a fearsome tug-of-war with their branches. The old maple creaked in protest and writhed and wriggled but couldn't loosen the wind's grip.

CRAAACK.

The maple gave a last despairing cry, crashed over the woodshed, and fell silent.

"My tree," sobbed Solomon the next morning. He ran through the rain and hugged the fallen trunk. "She was my friend…now she's gone…and I never said goodbye."

All that day Solomon's family worked. Father used the chainsaw to buck up the fallen trunk. Uncle burnt the branches scattered over the driveway and fixed the woodshed. Mother and Solomon stacked the maple logs inside.

Father handed the last log to Solomon and took him to stand in front of Uncle.

"Would you like to see the spirit of your special tree?" Uncle asked.

Solomon nodded.

"Tomorrow we'll start a mask together."

The next day Solomon carried the log to Uncle's workshop. Uncle swung the axe and split it straight down the middle. Solomon clutched half the log to his chest. He closed his eyes and thought about his tree. Uncle picked up his drum and began to dance and sing.

Gwā eee dim haoou,
Here is what I have to say:
Today we begin a carving.
We invite our ancestors to guide us,
To show my nephew the spirit of this special tree.
We honour our ancestors and thank them for their help.

Uncle's voice rang out. His drumming filled the clearing and rose to the sky.

Solomon's voice was small and his feet sad and heavy, but as his Uncle drummed, Solomon grew braver. He sang his own song.

Gwā eee dim haoou,
Here is what I have to say:
Tree, let your spirit guide Uncle's fingers,
Let those fingers show your face,
Let your face help my memory,
Let my memory always honour you.

Solomon took the pencil and marked the centre ring at each end of his log. Uncle drew a line through the middle and measured on each side.

The chainsaw whirred and sawdust flew as Uncle made the first cuts. Day by day the log transformed.

"Tell me about your tree," said Uncle as he planed the angles of the face. "What did you see among the branches?"

Solomon described the hummingbird nest and the antics of the baby birds. Uncle rounded the brow with the adze, chipped the hollows of the eyes, and told the hummingbird story.

"Did your tree smell nice?" asked Uncle as he used the hook knife to carve the nose.

Solomon remembered the sweet spring smell of sap and the pungent fall odour of crushed leaves. Uncle told of fall mushroom gathering in his grandmother's village.

"Did your tree have a voice?" asked Uncle as he showed how to carve the mouth.

Solomon told of whispered secrets and nightly lullabies. Uncle taught Solomon a family song.

"Is my mask finished now?" asked Solomon.

"Not yet. A mask needs to be worn. We must make room for your face. Careful...stand back," warned Uncle. He thinned out the back of the mask with the tip of the chainsaw. Then he showed Solomon how to hollow the nose and cheeks. Solomon helped scrape and chip. Shavings curled and the mask became thin and beautiful, a face to wear over a face.

Solomon was in charge of drying the mask. He stood on a chair and placed it in the microwave.

"Three times, at three minutes," he said, "with lots of turns."

They smoothed and sanded and rubbed and stroked until the face glowed under their fingers and began to look alive.

"Now what?" asked Solomon.

Uncle drew a hummingbird design across the smooth wooden forehead. Next he chose a tiny brush and began to paint. First the beak, then an eye and a face, finally a wing feathering across the brow. Last he painted the outline of the mask's lips and eyeballs, and very, very carefully Solomon filled them in.

When the paint was dry, Solomon oiled the mask. The wood sprang to life and smiled up at him.

"Hello, tree," whispered Solomon.

"Hello, Solomon," the mask whispered back.

By now a hint of spring was in the air. Solomon and his uncle walked outside into the pale sunshine. The cedars rustled a welcome.

"Mother, Father," shouted Solomon. "Come and see."

Uncle drummed and everyone sang as Solomon lifted the mask to his face and danced. Beneath their feet the spring sunshine warmed the ground and woke a dormant maple seed. As Solomon danced above, the tip of a root sprouted below and pushed into the loamy earth.

"Ahhh," whispered the cedars to each other. "A new beginning."

**Victor Reece**, Tsimpshian master-carver, created this mask for the story "Solomon's Tree." He also provided designs to Janet Wilson for the panels that appear at the bottom of some pages.

## DIG DEEPER

1. With a partner, role-play the scenes in the story when Solomon and his uncle work together to make the mask.

2. Write a sensory poem about a habitat that you know. Write two lines using each sense. Choose words that will create vivid pictures in the reader's mind.

# Connect and Share

You have discovered and learned interesting information and new ideas about habitats.

Now it's your turn to research and share information.

## Plan a diorama!

- Find a habitat in your community. Choose a local habitat, such as a ravine, park, or your backyard.

- Visit the area with an adult and gather information about the plants and animals you see.

## Create a diorama!

- Use a shoebox or other container in which to create your local habitat.

- Use modelling clay, play dough, and found materials to build the habitat.

- Design a sign for your diorama.

- Display your habitat for your classmates and invite them to ask questions about it.

# Spotlight on Learning

## Select

- Choose two pieces of work that show how you achieved the Learning Goals. (The same piece of work can show more than one goal.)

## Tell about your choices

- Tell what each piece shows about your learning.

| My choices | I want this in my portfolio because... |
|---|---|
|  |  |

## Collect

- Gather your research notes, brochure, diorama, and other work you did in this unit.

## Talk and Reflect

- Work with a partner.
- Together, read the Learning Goals on page 116.
- Talk about how well you met these goals.
- Look through your work for evidence.

## Reflect

- What have you learned about reading, researching, and sharing information about science topics?
- What new information have you learned about the survival of natural habitats?

177

# Acknowledgements

Permission to reprint copyrighted material is gratefully acknowledged. Every effort has been made to trace ownership of all copyrighted material and to secure permission from copyright holders. In the event of any questions arising as to the use of any material, we will be pleased to make the necessary corrections in future printings.

## Student Book

### Photographs

**Cover t** Brian Summers/Firstlight, **b** Wolfgang Kaehler/CORBIS; **2–3** © Don Mason/CORBIS; **8 clockwise**: Excerpt from *Kids with Courage: True Stories About Young People Making a Difference* by Barbara A. Lewis © 1992. Used with permission of Free Spirit Publishing Inc., Minneapolis, MN, 1-866-703-7822, www.freespirit.com, All rights reserved; Merna Forster, heroines.ca, A Guide to Women in Canadian History; Cover of *Maurice Ruddick Springhill Mine Survivor* by Joanne Stanbridge, © 2005 Pearson Education Canada Inc., Don Mills, ON, All rights reserved; CBC Original Pictures, www.cbceds.ca; **9** Olivier Ribardiere/Getty Images; **10** CP/Regina Leader Post—Roy Antal; **11 t** Royalty Free/Firstlight, **b** Roy Antal/Regina Leader Post; **12** Amanjeet Chauhan; **13** Amanjeet Chauhan; **14** CP/Hans Deryk; **ii r**, **15** International Olympic Committee, Switzerland; **16 t** Michael Goldman/Getty Images, **b** Olivier Ribardiere/Getty Images; **17** Olivier Ribardiere/Getty Images; **18** © David Watt Photography; **19** Comstock/ Jupiter Images; **20** © Wendy Bigcharles, **21** © Lonely Planet Images, **inset** © Wendy Bigcharles; **iii**, **22–26** photos courtesy of the Ecclestone family; **27** © Daniel Templeton/Alamy; **28 l** © David J. Phillip/Pool/ Reuters/CORBIS, **r** Photodisc/Getty Images; **28–29** Jim Reed/Firstlight; **29 l** AP Photo, **r** Toronto Star/Firstlight; **30** Adam Pretty/Getty Images; **40** Photodisc/Getty Images; **ii l**, **41** DK Images; **42** Michael Goldman/ Getty Images; **43** Lisa Pines/Getty Images; **54** Robert Manella/Getty Images; **55 t** Brad Wilson/Getty Images, **b** Seth Joel/Getty Images; **56–57** © Claudia Uribe Touri/Alamy; **62** Ray Boudreau; **64 bl** David Young-Wolff/Getty Images, **br** CP/Kingston Whig Standard-Ian

National Geographic Image Collection; **128** Oxford Scientific Films/ Firstlight; **129 t** © Peter Johnson/CORBIS, **b** A.G.E. Foto Stock/ Firstlight; **130 t** Rubber Ball/Jupiter Images, **b** Brand X/Jupiter Images; **131** Ray Boudreau; **132** GOODSHOOT/Jupiter Images, **inset** CP/Toronto Star/Tony Bock; **133** Jany Sauvanet/Photoresearchers/Firstlight, **inset** Nova Scotia Leatherback Turtle Working Group; **134 t** © Photo Researchers/CORBIS, **b** Photo by Denise Helferty; **135 t** Photo courtesy of National Aboriginal Achievement Foundation, **b** Photos.com/Jupiter Images; **136** Imagestate/Firstlight; **ix**, **137 t** © Steve Kaufman/CORBIS, **b** Marcus Pollard, Clifton Finch Aviaries; **138 t** Darwin Wiggett/Firstlight, **m** © Doug Wilson/CORBIS, **b** Darren Bennet, maXximages.com; **139 t** © Gary W. Carter/CORBIS, **m** © Hans Reinhard/zefa/CORBIS, **b** © Eric and David Hosking/CORBIS; **140 t** Frans Lemmens/Getty Images, **t inset** © GOODSHOOT/Alamy, **b** © Erskine/Alamy; **141 t** Digital Vision/Getty Images, **m** Jupiter Images/Photo Objects, **b** © Simon Murray Papilio/ CORBIS; **142** Ray Boudreau; **143** Ray Boudreau; **144** Photodisc/Getty Images; **144–145** Kelly Cannell and Susan Point, design for utility hatch cover, 2004, courtesy the City of Vancouver; **145** Anne Delaney; **150 t** Bruce Coleman Collection/Firstlight, **b** DK Images; **151 t** Douglas Faulkner/Photoresearchers/Firstlight, **b** © Clive Druett; Papilio/CORBIS; **152 t** Photodisc/Getty Images, **b** Oxford Scientific Films/Firstlight; **153** © Martin Harvey/CORBIS; **154–155** Reprinted with permission from the Canadian Wildlife Federation www.cwf-fcf.org; **176** Ray Boudreau; **177** Ray Boudreau

## Illustrations
**ii**, **4–7** Diane Dawson Hearn; **13** Photodisc/Getty Images; **15** Crowle Art Group; **19** Crowle Art Group; **20** Crowle Art Group; **iii**, **31–39** Dean Griffiths; **iii**, **44–53** © Robert J. Blake; **vi**, **58–61** Fraser Hallett; **83–84** Mary Wallace; **93** Anna Grossnickle Hines; **94** Lisa Desimini; **vii**, **96–104** Peter H. Reynolds; **vii**, **105–112** Colin Backhouse; **viii**, **124** Jeff Dixon; **125** Jeff Dixon; **viii**, **126** Jeff Dixon; **viii**, **128** Jeff Dixon; **137** Jeff Dixon; **146–149** copyright © 1992 by Lannis Temple; **152** Photodisc/Getty Images; **ix**, **156–165** Celia Godkin; **ix**, **166–175** Janet Wilson

## Text
"Mia's Problem" (original title "Black Thursday") from *More If You Had to Choose, What Would You Do?* by Sandra McLeod Humphrey, pp. 57–60 © 2003, Prometheus Books, Amherst, NY. Copyright © 2003 by Sandra McLeod Humphrey. Reprinted with permission; "Catch A Dream" from *Dream Catchers: The Climb of Two Natives* by CTV.ca News Staff;

# Shared Posters

## Photographs

**Poster 1:** James A. Sugar/Black Star © National Geographic Image Collection; **Poster 2: tl** Jeffrey Greenberg/Photoresearchers/Firstlight; **t inset** KEVIN AITKEN/Peter Arnold, Inc.; **rt** David R. Frazier/Photoresearchers/Firstlight; **rb** M.Wanner/UNEP/Peter Arnold, Inc.; **bl to r**: Dynamic Graphics/Firstlight; Eri Morita/Getty Images; John Warden/Getty Images; **Poster 3: l** Digital Vision/Getty Images; **tr** Digital Vision/Getty Images; **br** © Royalty-Free/CORBIS

## Illustrations

**Poster 1:** Photodisc/Getty Images; **Poster 3:** Jeff Dixon

## Text

**Poster 1:** "Across the Ocean Alone" from *Should Young People Set Daring Achievement Records?* Text by Walter Roessing. © 1997 National Geographic Society. All rights reserved.